Best of Luck
on Your Retirement
Howard

From the Staff
Saskatoon D.O.
June 22, 1993

A Pictorial History

Edited by D. H. Bocking
for
the Saskatchewan Archives Board

Western Producer Prairie Books, Saskatoon, Saskatchewan

Copyright © 1979 by the Saskatchewan Archives Board
Western Producer Prairie Books
Saskatoon, Saskatchewan
Second Printing 1980
Third Printing 1981

Cover and book design by Ray Statham

The publisher acknowledges support of this publication by the Potash Corporation of Saskatchewan

Printed and bound in Canada
by Modern Press
Saskatoon, Saskatchewan

Western Producer Prairie Books publications are produced and manufactured in the middle of western Canada by a unique publishing venture owned by a group of prairie farmers who are members of Saskatchewan Wheat Pool. Our first book in 1954 was a reprint of a serial originally carried in *The Western Producer,* a weekly newspaper serving western Canadian farmers since 1923. We continue the tradition of providing enjoyable and informative reading for all Canadians.

Canadian Cataloguing in Publication Data

Bocking, D. H., 1925-
Saskatchewan, a pictorial history

Includes index.
ISBN 0-88833-017-0 bd.
ISBN 0-88833-042-1 pa.

1. Saskatchewan - History - Pictorial works.
I. Saskatchewan. Archives Board. II. Title.
FC3511.B63   971.24'0022'2   C79-091210-4
F1072.B63

Contents

Foreword

To those familiar with the available publications on the history of Saskatchewan, the need for a new, comprehensive history of the province appears self-evident. The most recent general history, *Saskatchewan: The History of a Province* by J. F. C. Wright, was published in 1955 under the auspices of the Saskatchewan Golden Jubilee Committee. This volume, which is now out of print, was an important source for years. But historical perspectives change. Events, new research, and the discovery of additional historical sources by our archives and museums require each generation to reinterpret its past.

The proposal to publish a two-volume history of Saskatchewan to mark the province's 1980 Diamond Jubilee was developed by the Saskatchewan Archives Board. Formed in 1945, the Saskatchewan Archives Board is a joint endeavor, involving the Government of Saskatchewan, the University of Saskatchewan, and the University of Regina. Over the years, the Archives Board has been actively involved in seeking out, preserving, and encouraging the use of the documentary evidence concerning provincial history. The word "archives" often brings to mind images of old and dusty documents used only by scholars. But, as the many local historians, teachers, students, genealogists, journalists, television producers, and others who have drawn on the Saskatchewan Archives have found, a modern archives is very much a part of its community. An archives mirrors its society, with its collections reflecting all aspects of community life, providing a living, growing resource to be drawn on by all segments of society. Countless individuals

and organizations across the province have assisted the archives in ensuring the preservation of our documentary heritage. Through the publication of its journal, *Saskatchewan History,* the Archives Board has also encouraged the careful exploration of themes and topics in provincial history. The publication of a new history of Saskatchewan is in large part a report on the cumulative results of these archival efforts.

The history of Saskatchewan is complex and no one approach is sufficient. Recognizing this, the Saskatchewan Archives Board planned this history as two complementary volumes of which *Saskatchewan: A Pictorial History* is the first. The second volume, a full interpretative history of the province, has been entrusted to Dr. John Archer, President Emeritus of the University of Regina. In the spirit of free intellectual inquiry, the Archives Board has left decisions on historical content and interpretation entirely to the judgment of the authors. Together, the two volumes will draw on all forms of historical evidence to explore the full course of human development in the area now known as Saskatchewan.

Many individuals and institutions have participated in the preparation of this history over the past three years. The project was the first to be approved and begun for Celebrate Saskatchewan 1980 and full funding was provided by the provincial government through the Saskatchewan 1980 Diamond Jubilee Corporation and the Saskatchewan Archives Board. The ministers responsible for Celebrate Saskatchewan, the Honorable N. Shillington and the Honorable E. L. Tchorzewski, together with their staff, provided excellent co-operation. The University of Regina, the University of Saskatchewan, Saskatchewan Continuing Education, and Saskatchewan Culture and Youth assisted greatly at various times in the project. Successive chairmen of the Saskatchewan Archives Board, the Honorable D. L. Faris, the Honorable H. H. Rolfes, and the Honorable D. McArthur, have also given their full support to the history. In this they have been ably assisted by the other members of the Archives Board, Dr. Norman Ward (vice-chairman), the Honorable E. L. Tchorzewski, Miss Christine MacDonald, and Dr. B. Zagorin.

Ian E. Wilson
Provincial Archivist

Preface

This book is a pictorial history of the geographic area known today as the province of Saskatchewan. In the brief time that the region has been a part of Canada, it has undergone dramatic and fundamental changes. A highly mechanized, agricultural economy has developed where a buffalo-and-fur-trade economy once existed. Nomadic Indian encampments have been replaced by cities, towns, and villages, linked together by a complex network of roads and railways. Saskatchewan has become the home of diverse peoples, representing different racial, cultural, and religious groups. Both its society and government have grown and developed in complexity to meet changing needs. The development of the province has been affected by participation in two World Wars and by a shattering drought and depression, which caused widespread unemployment and social unrest. The illustrations and text which appear in this book have been selected to represent some aspects of these developments.

For the purposes of the present study, photography has provided the main documentation, but drawings, cartoons, broadsheets, pamphlets, and newspapers have also been used. Appropriate textual material from diaries, letters, reminiscences, travelers' accounts, books, and other publications has been used to augment the story told by the pictures. The textual material is not intended either to provide a full history of the particular event or scene depicted nor, in its totality, to take the place of a narrative history.

There are many ways of looking at the past, and the point of view of the writer or historian will determine what kind of history is produced. The medium used to tell the story also has a profound effect on the result. The decision to tell the history of Saskatchewan with visual material and brief quotations from written documents imposed very definite limits. The reader will not find here a definitive or analytical history of Saskatchewan. While in the main a chronological arrangement has been followed, it has not been possible to show all of the developments of our history. This volume is intended to be a companion volume to an analytical, narrative history of Saskatchewan. When read in conjuction with its more orthodox companion, it is hoped that it will add to the readers' understanding of our past.

Photographs are historical documents in the same way that letters, diaries, and business and government records are. In researching for this book, every effort has been made to establish the authenticity of each photograph, but it must be admitted that in many cases it has not been possible to do so because little is known about the provenance of some of the photographs. Repeatedly, for example, I have had to report in the picture credits that the photographer is unknown. Often little is known about the circumstances under which a picture was taken. Some interesting pictures could not be included, because the available information about them raised enough doubts to make their use unacceptable. Other pictures have been accepted and used in spite of incomplete information, because the facts available led to the conclusion that they were valid historical documents.

The history of photography in Saskatchewan remains to be written and is a separate study in itself. A significant number of photographs have survived and are in archival institutions, libraries, museums, and private collections. This suggests that many more pictures have probably been lost or are unknown to researchers. Still, when it came to choosing the comparatively few photographs that could be included in this book, the number of photographs available was daunting and the selection difficult. Photographs must offer information or evidence if they are to be used in a history. While availability was obviously a determining factor in making a choice of pictures, many fine, technically excellent photographs had to be left out because they did not, in my judgment, make a significant contribution to the story I was trying to tell. Such decisions are subjective and reflect the author's biases.

Saskatchewan's photographers have had their biases, too. They have tended to be interested in the new, the unusual, the special event, and not in the ordinary things of life which all of us share. Consequently the photographs that are available may present a somewhat unbalanced view of the past. It also must be remembered that, for technical reasons, most of the earlier pictures had to be posed, and they are therefore to some degree artificial. The photographs that have survived are probably those that pleased the photographer or those who were being photographed, whether or not they were closest to the truth. Anyone who has gone through the agony of selecting the one portrait proof he wants to have printed is well aware of this problem of selectivity. It must be recognized, then, that photographs, no matter how impeccable their credentials as historical records, record only an instant in time, and they may not record that instant entirely truthfully. They are useful historical documents, but they must be used with a knowledge and understanding of their limitations.

The camera cannot record everything, and there are historical developments and events which may be of considerable importance but which are difficult, if not impossible, to photograph. Social and political movements and the mood of a period, for example, are difficult to capture on film. The struggle for responsible government in the North-West Territories comes to mind as something that could not be recorded photographically in any meaningful way, and yet it was a movement of considerable importance in our history. A visual history for this reason is limited in what it can show, and in many areas it can only hope to be representative and suggestive.

There is some thanking to do, and I welcome the opportunity to acknowledge the assistance I have received from a number of individuals and institutions. Special thanks are due to Roxane Pelletier and Colleen Fitzgerald who worked as research assistants on the project and assisted in all phases of the work. Their dedicated work and personal interest in the project contributed considerably to its successful completion. Mrs. Kathlyn Szalasznyj joined the project at a later stage as a research assistant and helped in the selection of the textual material and in the detailed checking necessary to ensure its accuracy and uniformity. Lloyd Rodwell helped in compilation of textual material, the writing of captions, and the checking of sources. D'Arcy Hande contributed by doing some of the camera work that was necessary in the preparation of the photographic copies. The typing of the text was done by Mrs. Debbie Armstrong who managed to remain cheerful through the innumerable revisions and changes. The Regina staff of the Saskatchewan Archives Board and of the Saskatchewan History Project also assisted. Mrs. Jean Goldie, who is in charge of the photograph collection, and her assistant, Mrs. Janet Stoll, helped guide the initial selection of material, arranged for copy work, and provided information on the provenance of the photographs. Their constant willingness to help was of great assistance in the preparation of this study. E. C. Morgan, Trevor Powell, Ruth Dyck, Claudia Cunnington, and Endl Crane of the Regina staff of the Saskatchewan Archives Board assisted in the selection of textual material as did Dr. J. H. Archer, Jean Larmour, and Don Herperger of the Saskatchewan History Project.

I am pleased also to acknowledge the help received

from a number of institutions. These include the staff of the National Photograph and National Art collection, Public Archives of Canada; the United Church Archives, Toronto; the Notman Photograph Archives, McCord Museum; the Public Archives of Manitoba; the Hudson's Bay Company Archives; and the Glenbow-Alberta Institute. Help was also gratefully received from the following Saskatchewan institutions: the Archives Department, Moose Jaw Public Library; the Local History Room, Saskatoon Public Library; the Biggar Museum and Gallery; the Western Development Museum, Saskatoon; the Soo Line Museum, Weyburn; the Royal Canadian Mounted Police Museum, Regina; the Fort Battleford National Historic Park; the Maple Creek Museum; the Saskatchewan Wheat Pool; the *Leader-Post*, Regina; the Regina Chamber of Commerce; the North Saskatchewan Regiment, Saskatoon; the Tree Nursery and Experimental Farm, Indian Head; the Porcupine Plain Museum; the Co-operative College of Canada; and the University of Saskatchewan Archives.

Special thanks are due to the following individuals who made available their personal photographs, some of which we were able to include in the book: Mr. W. W. Aikenhead, Mr. Robert W. Anderson, Miss Evelyn Ballard, Mrs. Janet Barber, Mrs. Gertrude A. Barnsley, Mrs. Christina Bateman, Mrs. Joseph Bentley, Mr. E. E. Bidwell, Miss S. Carter, Mrs. Mary Cheney, Mrs. Gladys Clark, Mr. H. J. Cox, Mr. R. H. Crone, Mrs. B. A. Davidson, Mrs. N. L. Dering, Mrs. J. L. Donegan, Dr. Ian Dyck, Mrs. Lucy Eaton, Mr. J. M. Elliot, Mr. and Mrs. W. Forgay, Mrs. Ella Fraser, Mr. Alf Galenzoeski, Mrs. Art Grasser, Mrs. W. Hannerlindl, Mrs. Elaine Harrison, Mrs. Lula Hartsook, Mr. Lawrence E. Hauta, Mrs. R. Hawkins, Mr. B. Heibert, Mr. Dennis P. Herring, Isabelle Hoarsma, Mrs. Frank Hollick, Mrs. Joseph Hostyn, Mrs. Lillian Kallio, Mr. C. C. King, Mr. A. O. Lepine, Mr. H. A. Lewis, Edna Lifeso, Mrs. Phyllis Lunden, Mrs. D. Matheson, Mrs. V. Mathison, Mr. Theodore Matt, Miss A. McKay, Mr. and Mrs. G. L. McLeod, Mrs. Rose Melville-Ness, Mr. R. Monkhouse, Mr. E. Morris, Ida E. Morris, Mrs. Sidney Muri, Miss H. M. Purdy, Mrs. Sybil Rugg, Mrs. Margaret Salmond, Mr. Mike Siermacheski, Mrs. W. J. Smith, Mrs. Rose Stanek, Mr. R. G. Stebbings, Kay Stonehill, Mr. James Tingey, Mrs. A. C. van Nes, Mr. W. E. Veals, Mrs. K. M. Walberg, Mrs. Alvin Waite, Mrs. Edith Woolliams, and Mrs. Gertrude J. Workman.

In processing the photographs we had the assistance of a number of laboratories. These include the Audio-Visual Services photographic labs at the University of Saskatchewan and the University of Regina; the Photo Arts Services, Executive Council, Regina; West's Studio, Regina, and Gibson Photo Limited in Saskatoon. Both Mr. Murray Gibson and Mr. H. G. West also made available some of their photographs for inclusion in the book.

We are grateful to the author and publisher for permission to quote from C. Stuart Houston, editor, *To The Arctic by Canoe, 1819-1821*, McGill-Queen's University Press, 1974.

The book could not have been prepared without the support of the Saskatchewan Archives Board who have sponsored the work. I also want to thank the provincial archivist, Mr. Ian Wilson, for his support in many ways throughout the project. Finally but by no means least I want to acknowledge the support that my wife, Merle, gave throughout the project.

Putting together a book such as this requires that many decisions be made, and it is not surprising that at times I have wondered whether I was making the right choice. Although I have had advice and assistance, I accept full responsibility for the shape the book has taken and for the selection of the photographs and text.

CHAPTER 1

Contact and Change

The Indians of the western plains were a roving, nonagricultural people who lived by the hunt and depended on the buffalo for most of the necessities of life. They had developed a social organization and religious beliefs appropriate to their hunting society. The horse, which the Indians acquired around 1750, became an essential part of their nomadic life, both in the hunt and as a beast of burden. While Europeans learned from the Indians, the white man's culture, brought in by the explorer, fur trader, missionary, and settler, had so great an impact on the native people that the Indian way of life was drastically changed.

Left, Big Bear's camp, Maple Creek, 6 June 1883

. . . the tents were made of buffalo leather from eight to fourteen skins in size, all sewn together and cut into correct pattern, then stretched on the same number of poles adjusted to form a cone. . . . An oval opening, nearly at the bottom of the seam is cut out to form an entrance, and to fit this, a stretched leather door is hung by strings. Some slight adjustment of the poles is necessary to make the covering tight; this is done from the inside, and the tent is ready for occupation. . . . In the centre is the fire. Robes and blankets are spread all around to sit on.

Robert Jefferson, memoirs[1]

Below, Cree Indian drummers and dancers near Moosomin, 17 June 1889

Right, Indian woman drying saskatoon berries, place and date unknown

Thursday, 30 [July, 1801]. Different kinds of berries are now ripe, such as strawberries, raspberries, and what the Canadians call paires, which the Natives denominate Mi-sas-qui-to-min-uck. . . . These berries, when properly dried by the sun, have an agreeable taste, and are excellent to mix with pimican. The Natives generally boil them in the broth of fat meat; and this constitutes one of their most dainty dishes, and is introduced at all their feasts.

Daniel William Harmon, journal[2]

Far right, Indian woman removing fur from a hide, place and date unknown

The most valuable skin which the country produces, for clothing, is that of the moose deer. It is stretched on four sticks, and one side being elevated, several women mount upon it, with sharp instruments of iron or bone, scraping off in their descent, the hair and adhering flesh. . . . They next dry and then rub it, with a mixture of the brains and other parts of animals, after which, it is soaked in warm water and scraped, alternately, and smoked over a fire of decayed wood, which prevents it from becoming hard when it has been wet; for it absorbs water immediately. No skin is more durable or agreeable to the touch. . . .

Robert Hood, journal[3]

Below, *Buffalo Hunters Camp, 1858.* Watercolor by G. Seton, from a sketch by W. H. Napier, based on his recollection of the Canadian government exploring expedition which toured the West in 1858. At that time, the satisfaction of physical needs depended to a large extent on the success of the buffalo hunt. Buffalo meat was a major part of the diet of the fur trader, as well as of the Indian and Métis. Hunters' camps were a colorful sight on the prairies as nomadic hunters prepared to reap the wild harvest.

Here I saw my first hunting camp and a curious sight it was to me. . . . They always camp in a ring. Each hunter has on an average four or five carts. These are placed in a ring and they generally sleep under them except when lying in one place which is seldom as the refuse meat makes such an obnoxious smell that they move every three or four days. The ring here was about half a mile in circumference. Inside the ring the

horses are kept at night and grass cut and given them as the number of horses eat the ring bare in a few minutes.

W. E. Traill, 1865[4]

Right, Fort Carlton, established in 1795, was one of many inland posts built by the Hudson's Bay Company. Located at the junction of major land and water transportation routes, the post was designed to meet the trading needs of the local Indian population. The operations of the post called for the co-operative efforts of many employees. Of great value to the post were the Métis, who served as interpreters in carrying on trade with the Indians. As settlement and agriculture pushed back the fur frontier, Fort Carlton rose to prominence as a center for mail distribution, northern supply, conferences, and treaty payment. The fort was abandoned and accidentally burned in 1885, after serving briefly as a police post.

Below, half-breed traders, about 1872-1875

It must be remembered that within the last few years the half-breeds have been compelled to change their mode of obtaining a livelihood. Not long ago buffalo hunting and trading with the Indians afforded them a sure and easy method of living in luxury. As the buffalo disappeared they naturally turned to freighting. Supplies for the northern country and as far west as Edmonton came in to a large extent overland from Winnipeg, hundreds of miles distant. Freight was plentiful and prices high. The loss of the buffalo was not at the time severely felt. Freighting was second nature to them, and they did it wonderfully well.

A. B. Perry, Superintendent, North-West Mounted Police, 1887[5]

Below, the dock at Cumberland House, 1899. The men are carrying tea chests to load on board a York boat for shipment to the various posts of the Cumberland district, which in 1899 included The Pas, Cedar Lake, Grand Rapids, Pelican Narrows, Lac la Ronge, Lac du Brochet, Montreal Lake, Fort à la Corne, Portage la Loche, and Green Lake.[6]

There were ten men in the boat with 10,000 lbs. of freight. This freight used to come from Prince Albert for the Hudson's Bay Store. Then it was taken up north by these men for $1.50 a day and a ration of flour, tea and salt pork. . . . It took them 22 days to go from Cumberland House to Pelican Narrows and back to Cumberland.

Joe Pelly, A History of Cumberland House[7]

Below, Portage la Loche, 1908[8]
Upper right, Holy Trinity Church, Stanley Mission
Thursday, 6th [April, 1871]
   ... Daily morning and evening prayers [are held] in the church with exposition of a portion of God's word.... After service this evening I read the Lieutenant Governor's Proclamation respecting the transfer of the North West to Canada and explained to the people the altered prospects of the country and the necessity of being prepared for any changes that might be coming. I endeavoured to impress upon them that Christianity alone could preserve the remnants of their race from extinction.

Easter Sunday, 9th [April, 1871]
   Large congregations at both services and I feel sure that many entered with soul and spirit into the services. At Holy Communion several were in tears. 67 partook and the offertory amounted to £10-11. I feel often discouraged at seeing the empty pews Sunday after Sunday while my people are away at the hunting grounds but a sabbath like this day makes up for many discouragements.
                                    Rev. John Alexander Mackay
                                    at Stanley Mission, journal[9]

Lower right, church in the wilderness, Qu'Appelle Mission, no date

In 1870, Canada gained legal jurisdiction over the North-West. Three years later, the federal government created the North-West Mounted Police, to establish and maintain law and order in the recently acquired territories. The force was able to achieve good relations with the Indian people and to protect them and the white settlers from lawless elements. By their presence, the police also helped to establish Canadian sovereignty in the area. In addition, they assisted with the negotiation of a series of Indian treaties, through which the federal government hoped to assure a peaceful transition to agricultural settlement.

Upper left, drill order parade, North-West Mounted Police barracks, Regina, 1890

. . . [the Mounted Police] march in the streets and make a fine soldierly appearance. They are drilled. They practice firing at a mark. In a word they are being kept in a state of readiness for duty and the public is therefore getting value for the money spent on them.
Regina Leader, *25 October 1883*[10]

Lower left, North-West Mounted Police constable, Battleford district, about 1880

The [Mounted Police] came up and down the trail quite often in winter as well as summer. They nearly always stopped to see how the settlers were getting along, and if anything unusual was happening. We were always glad to see them and have a little talk to find out what was happening in the outside world.
Niels Gording, *remembrances*[11]

Right, the North-West Territories Council, Regina, 1884. Lieutenant-Governor Dewdney, who is at the head of the table in this picture, was appointed by the federal government and responsible to it. He was assisted by a council which in 1884 consisted of six members appointed by the government of Canada and eight elected members. Left side: C. B. Rouleau (standing), H. Richardson, D. H. Macdowall, Wm. White, J. H. Ross, J. G. Turriff; right side: Pascal Breland, J. F. Macleod, A. G. Irvine, F. Oliver, J. C. C. Hamilton, T. W. Jackson, J. D. Geddes. At the table to the right is A. E. Forget, clerk of the council. Absent: Hayter Reed.

Left, Geological Survey camp, Cold Water Coulee, Swift Current Creek, 1884. The Geological Survey of Canada was formed in 1842 to explore Canada. Its work included describing geological features, collecting specimens, fixing longitudes and latitudes, and publishing resource information. In 1868, the survey's work was extended to all the provinces of the Dominion, and an annual allocation of funds was provided to defray expenses. By the mid-1880s, photography became an integral part of the geological work, capturing and preserving prairie landscape, people, and wildlife with an animation hitherto unknown. Thomas Chesmer Weston (1832-1910) undertook four journeys into western Canada during the 1880s, paying special attention to the collection of vertebrate fossils and Indian artifacts from the Cypress Hills region.

All being ready we left Maple Creek at 12 noon, May 31 and struck off for the Cypress Hills, and our interesting fossil bone locality. . . . We made 18 miles that day and camped near a creek in close proximity to a large encampment of Blackfoot Indians who were engaged in collecting buffalo bones to be used for refining sugar and for fertilizing purposes. Continuing our journey the following morning, partly by trail and partly by compass we reached our field of research 48 miles from Maple Creek, Sunday, June 2nd — a great verdant valley extending many miles in a north and south direction.

Thomas C. Weston,
reminiscences[12]

Right, plan of Township No. 43, Range 1, West of the Third Meridian. By Orders-in-Council passed in 1869 and 1871 a system of surveys, which divided the land into townships containing thirty-six one-mile-square sections, was adopted for the lands in Manitoba and the North-West Territories. Most of the lands in Saskatchewan were surveyed according to these regulations, and the square sections shown on this plan were the usual pattern of survey. However, there were special exceptions. There were a few river-lot surveys as shown in this plan for the St. Laurent settlement. Lands for Indian reserves and Hudson's Bay Company reserves were also exceptions to the square-grid system of survey.

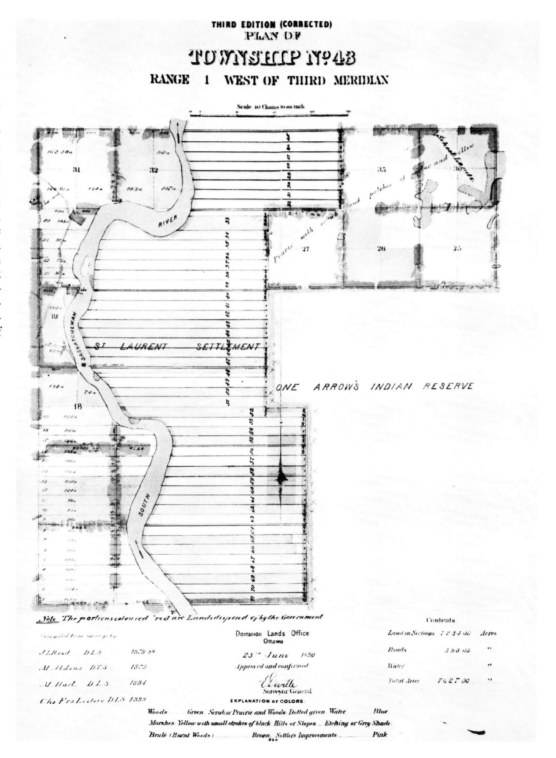

Below, Indian children with their fathers arriving at school, 1904. Left to right: James Keepness, Jessie Keepness, Jimmy Keepness, Tommy Notawasquitaway, Thomas Notawasquitaway. Jessie and Tommy had just arrived for enrollment in the Regina Industrial School, where Jimmy Keepness had already spent a year. The industrial-school system, which began operation in 1884, provided voluntary boarding schools for the education of Indian children throughout the West. The development of agricultural skills was the prime purpose of the schools. The assumption was that the Indians would make their living by farming in the future. Lands near the school were reserved for practical use; carpentry and harness-making were included in general farm classes. The girls were instructed in domestic skills.

With much trepidation I allowed myself to be handed over to the principal of the school . . . I shed no tear, but the pain in my heart was great, as I watched my father walking away. He did not look back once. I was much depressed, and scarcely noticed the boys kicking a football about the school grounds. Then two who were my cousins ran over and took charge of me. They had been in the school for more than a year, and they told me about it, persuading me to join in the game. In a short time, I forgot my troubles.   Edward Ahenakew, memoirs[13]

Below, Indian ploughing on a reserve in western Canada, place and date unknown

The great object of the Government is to turn the Indians of the prairies into farmers. Amidst many difficulties it must be said from a survey of these reserves [Qu'Appelle area] that the work is advancing. . . . One Indian, whose farm was visited, had very nearly fifty acres of wheat. It was well put in and presented an excellent appearance. It will probably yield between 800 and 1200 bushels of grain. If anyone doubts the capability of the Indian he has but to see this farm of a man who, ten years ago, lived by the chase to be convinced.

G. Bryce, 1885[14]

Below, advertisement for the York Farmers' Colony[15]. Special regulations permitting the sale of lands to colonization companies were passed by the Dominion government in 1881 to encourage the settlement of western Canada. One of the companies receiving a grant of land was the York Farmers' Colonization Company. The terms of the contract provided for a rebate of a portion of the sale price of the land to the company in return for establishing settlers. During the winter of 1882 advertisements such as the one shown here were circulated to recruit settlers.

This company experienced modest successes initially, but failed for a number of reasons, including the North-West Rebellion and the lack of railway branch lines. Nonetheless, its enterprise laid the foundation for the city of Yorkton and the settlement in the surrounding district.

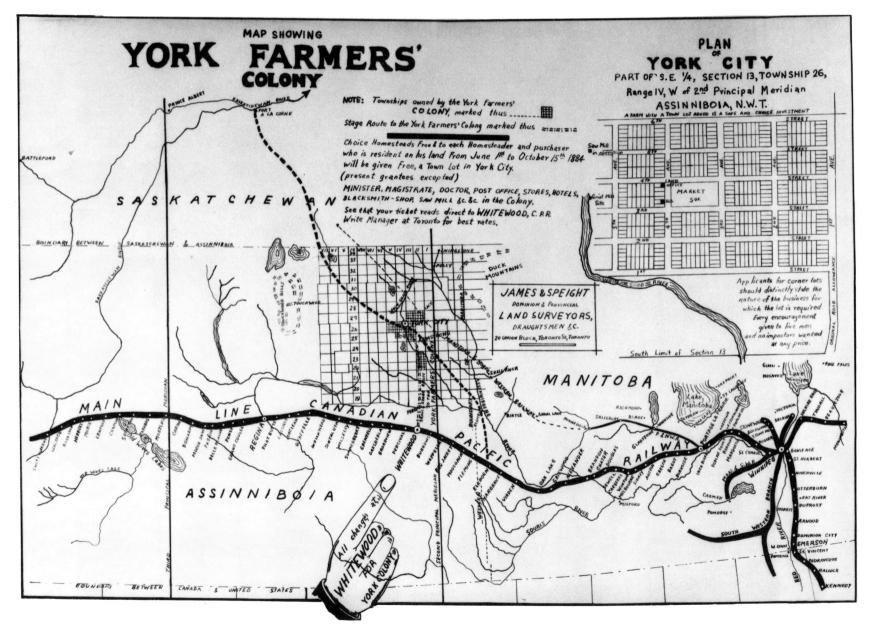

Below, Amos Kinsey farm, Moosomin district, about 1883

... I am glad that you are all pleased to hear of my getting another 160 acres by pre-emption, for it really is a fine thing, and it means a great deal ... half a section is just a nice cozy farm, and there is a good living in it for anybody, the independence of the thing is great ... I do not think that we should set our heart too much upon vanishing wealth and vain riches. I believe that a man should follow the life in which his soul can obtain the most rest and peace, and health and vigour for the body and that is my aim, a good home is the top of my ambitions, and that is why I like the life, it is the independence of the thing. I have hardly known what it means to be sick since I struck the West and to live a hand in glove life with nature, the green grain growing and developing, the beautiful sunsets we witness here, and the clear starrie nights, and above all, the grand immensity of the general surroundings illustrate the Almighty power of our creator, and humbles the pride of man, which sinks into nothingness before such vastness. ...

G. W. V. Yonge, reminiscences
of an early farmer[16]

The building of the railway, the virtual extinction of the buffalo, and the growing tide of white immigration threatened the Indian and Métis way of life. The Métis sought assurance from the federal government that their rights and lands would be protected. When the government failed to respond to their petitions, the Métis people invited their leader Louis Riel to return from the United States to help them seek redress of their grievances. Riel's attempt to force negotiations by taking up arms and forming a provisional government led to military conflict. The Canadian government rushed troops to the West and defeated the Métis forces. Louis Riel was subsequently tried and executed, and other leaders were imprisoned.

The four men pictured on this page were leaders of the Indians and Métis who took part in the rebellion. Those shown on the facing page were officers of the militia and police.

Upper left, Gabriel Dumont

Upper right, Louis Riel

Lower left, Chief Poundmaker

Lower right, Chief Big Bear

Upper left, Major-General F. Middleton, commander of the Canadian Militia and the North-West Field Force

Upper right, Lieutenant-Colonel W. D. Otter, Commander of the Battleford Column

Lower left, Lord Melgund, Chief of Staff, North-West Field Force

Lower right, Superintendent L. F. N. Crozier, North-West Mounted Police

Below, the *North West* at Battleford, 1885. Steamboats were first used on the Saskatchewan River in the 1870s and were an important link in the inland transportation system until displaced by the railroads in the 1890s. During the North-West Rebellion, steamers were used effectively to move men and supplies but the attempt to use the steamboat *Northcote* as part of the attack force at Batoche was a failure.

The steamer North West *arrived last evening at 8:15 o'clock, having left Prince Albert on Friday morning at 11. She had on board Gen. Middleton and staff, the Midland Battalion under Col. Williams, and Boulton's Mounted Infantry, one gun of "A" Battery, and Capt. Howard and his gatling.*

Captain Sheets was in command of the steamer, and having no pilot but himself, the double duty of wheel man and commander devolved on him.   Saskatchewan Herald, *25 May 1885*

Right, the trial of Louis Riel, Regina, 1885. On 6 July 1885 Louis Riel was formally charged with treason. Found guilty, he was hanged on 16 November 1885. His trial and execution had an important effect on Canadian politics as Riel became a symbol of the division between the major ethnic and racial groups in Canada.

Below, Half-Breed Claims Commission staff at the Trading House, Touchwood Hills, 1887. The commission was established to investigate and try to satisfy the land claims of half-breeds resident in the North-West Territories prior to 15 July 1870. It was authorized to enumerate the half-breeds and grant, where applicable, land or money scrip for the extinguishment of aboriginal title. The commission, headed by R. Goulet and N. Omer Coté, held sittings at sixteen places throughout the North-West Territories and Manitoba, and investigated 1,414 claims.

Right, Métis children at Ile-á-la-Crosse, 1908

CHAPTER 2

On to Saskatchewan!

Canada's acquisition of the Hudson's Bay Company lands in 1870 opened western Canada for development. The building of a transcontinental railway and the signing of treaties with the Indian populations were other essential preludes to settlement.

At first the rate of immigration was disappointingly slow and was further hampered by the North-West Rebellion of 1885. However in the period following 1896, a vigorous program was developed to attract settlers from elsewhere in North America and from Great Britain and the European continent. A flood of immigration literature was distributed to proclaim the fertility of prairie soils and explain the government's policy of free homesteads for agricultural settlers. Success was quickly achieved, as the immigrants came in their thousands.

Once the settler reached the West, he had to face the often formidable task of building a home and bringing his homestead land under cultivation. The large number of homesteads which were abandoned is evidence of the high rate of failure, but many of the newcomers succeeded, and within a comparatively short time Saskatchewan had become an important agricultural producer. The wheat economy had replaced the buffalo economy.

Left, crowd observing a working model of a Saskatchewan grain elevator, Canadian Emigration Offices, London, England, about 1912

... Jutting out close to the corner of Parliament street the Canadian Government offices face the historic open space of Trafalgar Square. ... That the more central position of the offices will serve Canada well is proved by the crowds who throng round the windows, and the bright and attractive nature of the buildings, will be emblematic to many of the bright future which Canada has to offer. ...

Department of the Interior annual report, 1904[17]

Left, leaving Liverpool for Canada, date unknown

After all the baggage had been taken on board the gangways were taken away and the people were allowed on the landing-stage near the ship. Thousands of people lined the stage, and about four o'clock as this great liner thronged with people all eager to catch a last glimpse of some friend, . . . the band played "Auld Lang Syne," and cheer after cheer rent the air. As the ship moved away from the stage the great crowd of people was seen to advantage, all waving handkerchiefs. It was a sight to move even the stoutest heart, and we all stood taking a farewell look until the crowd became but a speck in the distance.

Wm. Hutchinson[18]

Below, emigrants for Canada on a liner crossing the Atlantic, about 1913

The cabins were 7 feet square, with upper and lower bunks on 3 sides, and the door on the fourth side, and all below the water line. So you can guess we spent most of the time on deck. The grub was dished up in wash tubs and you helped yourself. . . . It took 12 days to make the crossing, and I want to tell you the North Atlantic is no place to be in April. . . . There was no privacy on a boat this size with 2000 people jammed together, but we got along ok.

Herman Collingwood, memoirs[19]

Below, Scottish immigrants aboard a train on their way west, date unknown

Special after special brings its multitude of eager hardy home-seekers. Freight trains, heavily laden with settlers' effects, crowd the tracks. The steamships leaving Europe for Canada are overcrowded, and many, unable to secure passage for Canada direct, come via New York and Boston. Still they come, and promise to come, their faces turned westward, where free farms are to be had.
"On to Canada!"

Regina Morning Leader, *27 April 1907*

2476

Below, interior of a colonist car, 1908

Our train consisted of several long coaches and looked huge compared to our English trains. Each coach has a long corridor down the centre with seats accommodating four on either side. The entire coach seated eighty-four passengers. At night the seat pulled together forming a sleeping place for two persons and the roof portion above pulled down making another berth for two. . . . At the end of each coach was a small apartment furnished with a stove for heating water and warming up food. Wash rooms and lavatories for both men and women were also provided. There were no mattresses for the berths and no privacy if you wished to undress when going to bed. It was rather embarrassing the first night, but after that the women either erected a blanket or pinned up sheets of paper. This method of travelling was quite novel to most of us but we soon got accustomed to it.

Hembrow F. Smith, diary[20]

Left, Dominion Land Office and Customs Office, Maple Creek, about 1906. To attract settlers to the vacant lands of the North-West Territories the government of Canada adopted a free homestead grant system by Order-in-Council in 1871. While there were subsequent changes in the legislation, the basic system remained the same. Entry for a homestead of 160 acres was permitted on the payment of a ten-dollar fee. In order to obtain title to the land, the homesteader was required to complete specific residence and cultivation duties. The homesteader registered for his land at the local Dominion Land Office. Settlers coming from the United States were allowed to bring certain settlers' effects free of charge but these would have to be cleared through the nearest Customs Office.

Right, lineup for land, Yorkton, 1907. When highly desirable areas were made available for homestead entry, land rushes sometimes developed. Not infrequently this led to long lineups at the local agency office by those anxious to register for one of the coveted homesteads. This lineup in Yorkton developed when lands formerly occupied by or reserved for Doukhobors were thrown open for entry.

On Friday morning, June 14, one of the choicest townships of the entire Doukhobor reserve was thrown open at the land office here to homestead-seekers and resulted in scenes of great excitement. . . .

At three o'clock a large crowd gathered which kept increasing until at six o'clock the street and sidewalk were both impassable and the police were almost powerless.

Yorkton Enterprise,
20 June 1907

"The Line-up"

Below, Barr colonists, Saskatoon, 1903. While most of the intending settlers arrived alone or in small family groups, some came as members of organized parties. The Lloydminster area was settled by English people who had been brought together by the Rev. Issac Barr. They traveled as far as Saskatoon by train but had to complete their journey in wagons.

In the course of the next week the camp [of Barr colonists at Saskatoon] was all bustle. Men were making purchases of horses, oxen, waggons, ploughs, food, etc. in preparation for the journey to the location of the land. Much money changed hands and it was rumoured some five hundred waggons, a thousand horses, cattle and oxen, eight hundred ploughs, 150 mowers and 50 binders had been sold to the settlers and it was also reported the Bank of Hamilton, the only small bank in the village, had cashed drafts for the colony members of over a quarter of a million dollars. Men in waggons could be seen all over the camp trying out their new horses and oxen, and not being accustomed to driving the latter, some very amusing incidents occurred. . . .

Hembrow F. Smith, diary[21]

Below, leaving Moose Jaw for the homestead, date unknown

We bought two hornless shorthorn oxen for $200.00 with harness consisting of leather collars which are put on the opposite to horse collars as the withers of the oxen is the widest part. . . . We also bought a sound used wagon, three sections of drag harrows with draw bar, walking plough, shovels, picks, crowbar, ten by twelve tent, camp cot, .22 rifle, cooking utensils, sheet iron camp stove, one burner primus stove and fuel, two tin three gallon milk cans with tap in bottom and transparent panel showing amount of cream when running off milk, a butter one pound print and wooden bowl to work butter in, a tin dash churn, large covered tin bowl for bread making and various kitchen utensils. We also bought a storm lantern and coal oil lamp, three 25 foot tether chains and last, but not least, a two year old recently calved cow bought from my late employer for $28.00. She supplied all our needs with surplus butter to trade in the store. As to food — 100 lbs. flour, 98 lbs. rolled oats, 100 lbs. sugar, 10 lbs. corn syrup and several pieces of home cured bacon from the same source as the cow. Thus equipped we started for our destination about thirty miles away.

Harry Self, memoirs[22]

Upper left, Doukhobors plastering a log house, place and date unknown

Lower left, sod and lumber home, built by Menno Moyer in the Redvers district, about 1900. Mr. Moyer began residence on his homestead in May 1900. His family consisted of his wife and eight children.

Upper right, Martin Larson's tar-papered log house with pole-and-sod roof near Preeceville, about 1912. Children are Inez, Bessie, and Milly.

Lower right, a barn made of poles and flax straw, on the homestead of John Porter (west 1/2 27-13-12 w.2), about 1906. Left to right: John Porter, Rev. David Irvine, Ed Porter, Israel Hoover, and Ora Porter. The people in the picture were members of the Brethren Church.

Upper left, the home of Mrs. Roseland, which served as the Landrose Post Office, located about ten miles north of Marshall, 1910

Everyone was anxious for a post office and school. My father worked hard for both, but found the post office the easier to get. When the government wrote for particulars, such as where he was born, etc., my father replied that he was born in Zorra, Ontario. To our surprise, when the post office equipment arrived in August of 1905 it was addressed to Zorra, Sask. — and thus it was named. . . . The post office became the centre of many attractions and gatherings. Saturday was mail day and the arrival of all the settlers would begin by 4 o'clock for this weekly event. They came in ox wagons, buggies, horseback and on foot from miles around. They often had to wait until dark and sometimes all night. I've seen them sleeping on the floor just in case the mail would arrive at any moment.

Yorkton Enterprise, *6 October 1955*

Lower left, a settler's shack near Lloydminster, 1906

In open spaces, loneliness must . . . [be intense]. In this parkland belt our spaces are small in comparison and there are so many things here to hold one's attention and occupy the mind. The first few years I spent alone, away in a poplar log shack. My nearest neighbor was located only seven miles to the north-west. In winter time if snow drifted badly it became impossible to keep in touch. One diversion from loneliness was found in keeping diaries on different subjects: weather, general conditions such as wind (velocity), clouds (density, form), rain (graduated measure), first and last fall of snow (dates, height); the number of wild life — deer, coyote, lynx, grouse, other animals and birds over an area. . . . Only once did I feel that oppressive power of absolute loneliness, that was when I endured for two weeks that painful affliction, snow blindness. My dog, Jock, a Husky, was a friend indeed — guided me to feed stock and would help bringing wood for the heater and stove, a guide, guard and friendly comforter, and asked for so little in return. They'll share your troubles, help you in difficulties to their last breath. All they ask is your kindly friendship. A man and his dog are never lonely, and he'll point you out things with his steady gaze you'd never see otherwise, oft times averting danger to one self. Once Jock saved my life in the worst blizzard I experienced here.

Charles Davis, *reminiscences*[23]

Right, sheep ranch near Moose Jaw, no date. The rancher, not the homesteader, laid first claim to the grasslands of southern Saskatchewan, often drawing on his experience of managing livestock on the American plains. In place of the buffalo which had once roamed the open range, cattle, horses, and sheep now grazed on lease lands. Riding the range often meant long hours of hard, lonely work which was far different from the romantic depiction of the life of a cowboy in contemporary literature.

Below, J. R. Warn Ranch, Reliance, date unknown

A good deal of more or less interesting literature has been written at one time and another dealing with the almost superhuman daring and the reckless deeds of the cow boy, but in actual practice he is found to be very much like his brother man, neither more daring nor less reckless, and, as a general rule, a sober, hard-working member of his own community.... round-ups signify work, and work too of a kind that is no sinecure for anyone connected with them from the captain down to the horse wrangler, as the gentleman in charge of the horse herd is named. What with bull round-ups, spring round-ups, beef round-ups, calf round-ups, fall round-ups; gathering the weak cows on whom the grim and heavy hand of winter is making itself felt; feeding the young weaners, doomed to their orphan lives, herding the bulls, all these, with many other duties too numerous to detail, fully occupy the lives of those who gain their daily bread by ranching in the Canadian Territories.

Anonymous[24]

J. R. WARN RANCH, RELIANCE, SASK.

Below, branding calves on the prairies, Horace Greeley Ranch, no date. Mr. Greeley established a ranch south of Maple Creek in 1890 and ranched there for many years.

The animals are each in turn roped (lassoed) by the hind-legs while on the run, and thrown by a man on horseback. This is an accomplishment which months and years of practice will never make you efficient at, if you do not acquire the knack readily after repeated attempts. It is a heaven-sent gift to any stockman, and too few in the cattle country can, in these days, lay claim to handling the "hard-twist" as it should be handled. Should you, my reader, be one of the favoured few, good luck to you! You will never want for a job at $30 a month the year round. The calf is then dragged by the rope (which is made fast to the horn of the Mexican saddle) to the fire, where a man should be ready to apply the irons to whatever part of the body is indicated on your brand certificate, while another man holds down the beast's head, and another one its flank.

A.B. Stock, memoirs[25]

In the grain lands, as on the ranches, calloused hands did much to win Saskatchewan for agriculture. Between arriving on the land and gathering the first crop lay many farm operations that demanded perseverance and hard work. Perhaps as important to the homesteader as good seed grain was his faith that land, climate, and other factors would work together to keep him on the land and that, eventually, title would be obtained to make the land his own.

Upper left, clearing land, Whitewood district, 1910

Lower left, breaking land with oxen and walking plow, St. Luke district, 1912

Right, Benjamin Smith plowing with a steam engine, Boharm, 1901

Below, horse-drawn seed drill being used on the farm of A.W. Lauder, Govan, date unknown

Right, haying, place and date unknown

Owing to the value and scarcity of labour, farmers and ranchers have contrived various expedients for getting the hay together with more or less success.

One such plan, where a stack is put up on the spot, is what is known as sweeping it. A beam of wood some twenty feet long, with a team of horses or bulls harnessed to each end, is used, and when it works well, will draw huge heaps together ready to be put into a stack.

Edward West, reminiscences[26]

Upper left, cutting the crop, place and date unknown

Lower left, setting up a binder, 1902: Enos Beach and his children assembling a binder for J. Mitchell

Right, thrashing on the farm of George Kidd, about 1906

The Canadian thrasherman is a sort of machine. He has little to say, just bolts down his food, and is up and off to his beloved engine. He seems only happy when enveloped in a cloud of smoke hurrying from the engine to look how the separator is running. Only do his features relax when he is surveying the busy workers around the stacks; he appears to have only one aim in life, and that is to see the neatly-built grain stacks converted into an untidy straw pile. . . .

This outfit was only a small one, but required twelve men to run it properly, and when you are having the thrashing outfit — well — it's a busy time. . . .

The men came back with the water tank, and placing it alongside the engine, commenced to fill the boiler . . . in about an hour's time the toot-toot of the whistle caused every man to hurry to his post.

Have you ever pitched big, heavy sheaves of grain for a thrashing machine? If not, I can tell you it is no soft job. . . .

William Hutchinson, 1906[27]

Left, John Matthiesen's new elevator, Estevan, about 1907. To promote the bulk handling of grain, the railway companies offered incentives to companies and individuals who would invest in building grain elevators alongside the tracks.

The vast increase in production on this Continent ... rendered obsolete the old methods of marketing and selling grain. ... Bulk handling was facilitated by the elevator, which took advantage of the flowing property of grain to make the force of gravity do what had formerly required a great deal of labor. This saving in labor was accompanied by an even greater economy of time; whereas it formerly required roughly a day to load a car from a wagon or from a flat warehouse without loading machinery, a car can be loaded from an elevator in fifteen minutes.

Undoubtedly this product of Yankee ingenuity is the most economical and most rapid method of handling grain that has ever been devised. ...

W.C. Clark,
The Country Elevator ...[28]

Right, dumping grain, 1900

We bagged our wheat in sacks; heavy cotton sacks which cost as much as thirty cents apiece for the heavier brands. At the elevator we dumped the contents of these bags through a kind of hatch into a hopper, where the elevator man would weigh it and give a ticket in exchange. This grain-cheque could be cashed in any bank or in most of the better stores. We used what was called the 'Manitoba knot' for tying these bags; a simple twist, or half-hitch, which would keep the bag tightly tied, but, at a tug of the mittened hand would untie easily. Fiddling with an unruly knot in zero weather is not a very nice job, and these little conveniences mean a great deal to the average working man.

In later years, grain was hauled in open wagon-boxes called grain tanks and I have often hauled over a hundred bushels in one tank with two good horses; but that was after I left the Qu'Appelle and its steep banks. Now, of course, with the march of progress, wheat is handled in heavy trucks with five or even ten ton capacity loads.

P. Crampton, memoirs[29]

Below, wheat blockade, Wolseley, 1901. Heavy yields, a late harvest, and a shortage of cars caused a "grain blockade," preventing the delivery of much of the grain crop before the close of navigation. Storage had to be found on the farm. Farmers complained of the congestion at the elevators, as well as of inconsistent grading and high service charges. These grievances were factors in the development of the Territorial Grain Growers' Association, through which producers hoped to remedy their grain-marketing problems.

In 1901 it was my house that Mr. Peter Dayman and I . . . drafted a letter to send to a number of farmers from Wolseley to Qu'Appelle, asking them to meet at Indian Head on a given date to consult as to what were the best steps to be taken in order to work out some remedy to existing conditions. . . .

We met at Indian Head and it was the same day [18 December 1901] that Premier Roblin and Premier Haultain were meeting in connection with boundary matters between Manitoba and the Northwest Territories. . . . I took advantage of the presence of [the] crowd; their meeting was at night and we called our meeting for the afternoon. Instead of about a dozen farmers there, as I had expected, the movement got noised abroad with the result that we had from sixty to seventy-five farmers there in addition to a number of public men.

At this initial meeting we decided to form what was called then 'Territorial Grain Growers' Association' and they appointed me as provisional President and John Millar of Indian Head was appointed provisional Secretary.

W.R. Motherwell, memoirs[30]

Right, W.R. Motherwell

Far right, Peter Dayman, 1903

Below, Thirteenth Annual Convention of the Saskatchewan Grain Growers' Association, Moose Jaw, probably Zion Church, February 1914. After the establishment of the Province of Saskatchewan in 1905, the Territorial Grain Growers' Association in Saskatchewan became the Saskatchewan Grain Growers' Association.

Every corner of the province had its representative present among the seven hundred delegates who constituted the convention and it was apparent that they were picked men who knew why they were present and what the association meant to them and their fellow farmers. . . . the large attendance generates greater enthusiasm and the delegates are able to become acquainted with a larger number of farmers from other parts of the province. . . . the world is watching these conventions and their conclusion as to the importance of the movement is liable to be judged in many quarters by the number of delegates in attendance quite as much as by the conclusions reached.

Grain Growers' Guide, *18 February 1914*

Below, Women Grain Growers of Saskatchewan executive, Regina, February 1918

The far-reaching effects of such an organization of women cannot be over-estimated. They came right from their kitchens to the convention and have demonstrated beyond debate that they are capable of performing valuable work for mankind outside the home which many men like to call their "sphere". When the business of the nation comes to be conducted in such a manner then it is a bad day for the nation. We wish the women every success in their organization.

Grain Growers' Guide, *18 February 1914*

For many of the early farm people, political involvement had other attractions besides the chance to improve economic conditions. The main meetings and conventions also brought a welcome respite from the routine of everyday life. The domestic life of the pioneer was marked, not by the hands of a clock, but by the regular calling of daily and seasonal chores. Much time was spent meeting the physical needs of the day and preparing for winter. These tasks called for the energies of the husband, the wife, and often the children.

Below, the MacLavertys, Battleford area, about 1905

Every family had a garden and grew melons, marrows and pumpkins as well as potatoes and other root crops to store in the cellars. The main annoyance was the mosquitos, and even the men wore mosquito netting over their heads and gloves on their hands. . . .

The children worked almost as hard as their parents. They walked, rode or drove two, three or even four miles to school. They helped with all the chores and work on the farm. They learned how to cope with emergencies. The training and hardship made them valuable citizens. . . .

Sylvia Mitchell, essay[31]

Upper right, Alec Howard, Whitewood, about 1915

Lower right, Corline Convery milking a cow, Ernfold, about 1923

. . . by and large these women were the salt of the earth. They worked such long hours with none of the amenities found in farmhouses today. They did the milking, separating, churning, baking, cleaning, washing — scrub board and maybe a wringer, otherwise by hand — no tattle tale grey ever came out of her wash-boiler. And what great meals and lunches she provided. She baked 10 loaves of bread every day except Sunday. Her kitchen stove was in constant use, summer or winter, for enormous baking sessions, heating the water in the reservoir attached to it, heating irons to do the ironing and pressing on Friday if there was a dance in the offing. Also it was a dandy place to sit with your feet up in the oven and . . . you could sit on the oven door to warm your posterior.

Ruth MacIntosh, memoirs[32]

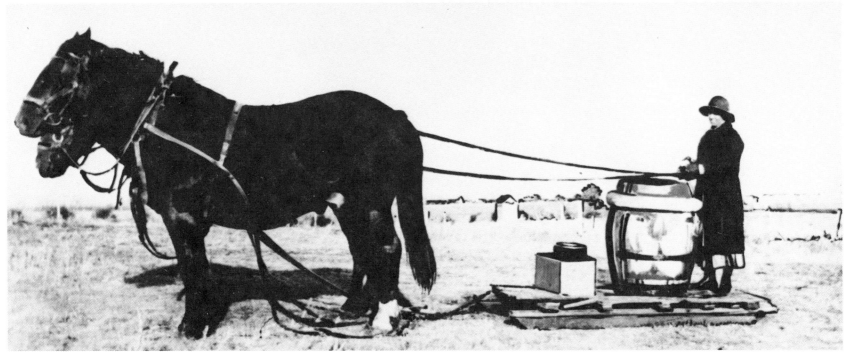

Upper left, W.G. Palmer, Mrs. Palmer, and David Wilkinson watering horses (Nancy and Lorna), Keddelston, about 1908

Unfortunately I cannot live on it [the homestead], since there is no water to be found. The cattle must be driven 4 or 5 miles to a watering place, and we have to go 5 or 6 miles for drinking water. I have hunted all over the homestead, and can find no water. What is the farm to me if I have no water.

We tried for water in 4 different places; 3 wells we went down 60 feet and one 106 feet without finding water. At the time of thrashing last fall we had to drive 30 miles for water to do our thrashing with.

Homestead records[34]

Lower left, Mrs. Violet McNaughton hauling water, Harris district, about 1909-1914

I remember that to get water Alf Murch who lived west of Abbey and south of Lancer, carried two pails of water on a yoke over his shoulders, from the spring north of Campbells to his place three and a half miles away. In the winter he melted snow for water. Others hauled water as far as eight to ten miles, either on a stoneboat or in barrels on a wagon. The people who had oxen would starve the animals down, until they got good and dry. The oxen would drink as much water as was in the barrels, this would be like taking two loads of water back, one load in the oxen and the other in the barrels.

Lars Larson, essay[33]

Right, rabbit hunter, possibly in the Peterson district, date unknown

Game was plenty. The rabbits sat around the haystacks by the dozens. If the doors were open they often ran in the house especially if the dogs chased them. They were so frightened they did not no [sic] where to go. One of our main dishes was rabbits. There was fried rabbit, stewed rabbit, rabbit ground into hamburgers, and smoked rabbit and rabbit everywhere winter or summer.

Minnie Taphorn, reminiscences[35]

Below, scraping a pig, date and place unknown

One morning early we were taken out of bed to go pig butchering at grandpa Wiens' place. We may have gone for breakfast, that was the style then. Father used a rifle on our hogs, some people still did it in the more primitive way with a knife. The pigs had to be scalded and scraped very clean, then washed, and the insides taken out. There was a long board table rigged up where the men cut the meat with sharp knives.

The women were busy at first, cleaning the entrails, those things had to be turned inside out, where they used a lot of warm water. . . . When they were ready to make sausages that was the time we liked to watch, they came out of the machine as if by magic. Liver sausage came next, they were made of the partly cooked jowls and the liver, then cooked for an hour or so. Things were cleaned up and every family went home with a small parcel of spare-ribs and liver sausage.

Sarah Friesen, reminiscences[36]

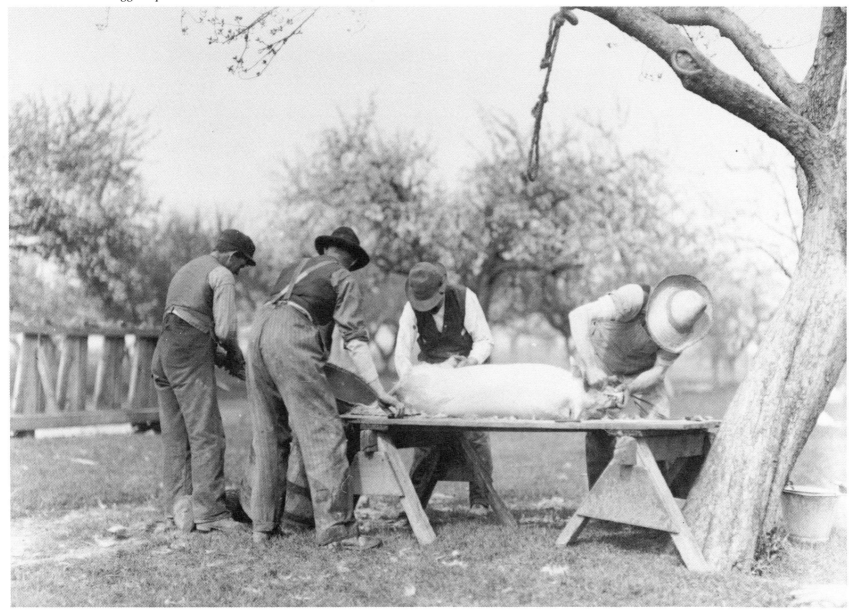

Right, Scandinavian settler, Hulda Swedberg, grinding coffee, Marchwell, 1906. Coffee beans were freshly ground before the coffee was made. This beverage was served about four times a day in many early Scandinavian homes.

We got from three to five meals a day and with an occasional letter and the latest paper, from two weeks to a month old, with the great big hope of a wonderful future of seas of golden grain, and the network of railways, [this] gave us strength to overcome the unsurmountable [sic] barriers in making a home . . . which called forth every oz. of physical strength we had to give. How did we do it? Baking dozens of loaves of bread, making our own butter, caring for chickens and turkeys, and gardens, milking cows, making our own soap, pickling our own pork for smoking and canning and preserving under almost primitive conditions, doing our own sewing for our family didn't leave much time for dreaming, and yet the dreams were there; engrossed in our homes, we accepted all that went with it. But always dreaming of better days to come.

*Mabel (Wilson) Hawthorne,
reminiscences*[37]

CHAPTER 3

Building a Society

Homesteading and pioneer farming were not the only developments in the early years of Saskatchewan. Along with agricultural growth there was the development of government at all levels. Cities, towns, and villages and a system of road and railroad transportation had to be built to service the farming areas and the industrial development that took place. Educational, medical, recreational, and cultural facilities were established to meet the needs of a society growing in population and complexity.

The first government of the North-West Territories consisted of a Lieutenant-Governor and an appointed council. By 1888 the council had been replaced by an elected assembly but the Lieutenant-Governor retained exclusive control over the expenditure of the annual Parliamentary grant to the North-West Territories. Between 1888 and 1897 the territorial assembly won control over finances and achieved responsible government, but the territorial government did not possess many of the rights and powers of a provincial government. In 1905 provincial rights were obtained by the creation of the provinces of Alberta and Saskatchewan.

Left, Sir F. W. G. Haultain (1857-1942), a leader in the struggle for responsible government and premier of the North-West Territories, 1897-1905

Right, Walter Scott (1867-1938), premier of the Province of Saskatchewan, 1905-1916

Upper left, Inauguration Day decorations, South Railway Street, Regina

Lower left, inauguration ceremonies for the Province of Saskatchewan, Regina, 4 and 5 September 1905. Seated left to right: Sir Wilfrid Laurier, Mrs. J.H. McIllree, Lady Grey, Earl Grey, Lady Laurier, Lieutenant-Governor Forget, remainder not identified.

The great, the long expected and much-prepared-for day has come and gone, and amidst much pomp and ceremonial and boundless popular enthusiasm Saskatchewan has taken her place in the confederation of Provinces that constitute the Dominion of Canada.

Regina Leader, *6 Sept. 1905*

Upper right, Legislative Building, Regina, about 1910

Lower right, Legislative Library, Legislative Building, Regina, 1913. Right to left: John Hawkes, legislative librarian; Robert W. Shannon, legislative counsel and law clerk; James P. Runciman, assistant to the legislative librarian; Mrs. H.B. Young, library assistant; Mr. W.H. Munro, assistant librarian; remainder unidentified

The long vistas of the graceful rooms is not interfered with as the shelving is along the walls; the floor space is very little encroached upon; the lighting is equally good for all the stacks, and all the books are equally accessible as the upper tiers are reached by light steel staircases leading to a gallery, with marble floor and brass hand railing, running the entire length.

Public Service Report, *1913*[38]

Even more important to the provincial government than the establishment of libraries and other cultural amenities was the provision of railway branch lines.

While the building of the main-line transcontinental railway had been essential to the opening of the West for settlement, branch lines were extremely important to the success of the individual pioneer. Pressure from both the settlers and the railway companies was placed on the provincial government to help in the construction of branch lines. Since the Dominion government had retained control over the public lands, the provincial government could not provide land grants to help in the construction of branch lines, nor could it afford to grant subsidies. Instead, in 1909, legislation was passed to permit the government to guarantee the bonds of railway companies for the building of approved branch lines. While this helped to get the lines built, it did not entirely resolve the government's problem, for the Legislature was often caught between the demands for branch lines and the railway companies' unwillingness or inability to build them.

Below, Canadian Pacific Railway track layer at work, Eastend, 1914

. . . here came the track laying gang. First a car of ties and then a car of rails. Each man grabbed a tie and laid it on the grade and then a gang of men on each side of the train picked up a rail. They carried it up front and laid it on the ties and 2 men bolted on the plates connecting them to the last one laid. The engineer went ahead with the width gauge and the gang drove in a spike every 10 ft. or so. The engine said toot and moved the cars up one length. The other gang came behind and drove in the rest of the spikes, and the Transcontinental had moved another length on it's [sic] way to the Pacific. Track laying in a nutshell.

Herman Collingwood, memoirs[39]

Right, the first train into Prince Albert, 5 September 1890. This railway was built with a federal land grant of 6,400 acres per mile and a subsidy totalling $1,000,000.

1ST TRAIN INTO PRINCE ALBERT. N.W.T. SEPT. 1890.

Upper left, Regina railway station, date unknown

Standing midway between Winnipeg and Calgary and in the centre of the richest portion of the great North American wheat belt, Regina, with railways already radiating from it to the four points of the compass, occupies a position of exceptional commercial strength. . . . with the rapid settlement of the new provinces the necessity arose for a centre less remote than Winnipeg to serve as a base of supplies, and Regina was marked out by geographical conditions and the railway engineer to fill that position. . . .

The city's commercial future as the chief distributing point for Saskatchewan was assured in 1902, in which year the C.P.R. first granted the shippers of the city a local freight tariff. . . . From that year the city as a wholesale centre has never for one instant looked back, and every year, every month indeed, sees new wholesale firms locating in the city and making it the distributing point for their western trade. . . .

Regina Morning Leader,
27 April 1907

Lower left, Canadian Pacific Railway station, Caron, about 1900

Right, railway station interior, Estevan, 1911

The country is greatly in need of more railway accommodation, and the evil will soon be much worse. For the first ten and a half months of 1902, 719 homestead entries have been made at the Saskatoon land office alone by bona fide settlers, besides all that have been made at other points along the line. Yet they are coming, and will all winter, in the greatest rush we have ever seen. Very greatly increased railway accommodation is absolutely and urgently required in more main lines, branches and rolling stock or our country and its fair prospects and opportunities will bleed at every pore.

Saskatoon Phoenix,
21 November 1902

Upper left, the growth of towns: Railway Avenue, Wawota, 1910

The coming of the railroad changed the pattern of living for the settlers south of the Pipestone Creek. For with the coming of the trains followed by the railway stations, station agents, section men, and section men's houses, a nucleus for a town was created encouraging general stores, hardware stores, blacksmith shops, lumber yards, and other commodity outlets and services to establish themselves at the rail stops, which were located at approximately eight mile intervals.

Alex Cunningham,
family history[40]

Lower left, Carlyle, 1903

Hammers could be heard day and night, all along Main Street as the freshly arrived merchants, hotel men, livery stable operators and the like worked furiously to get their premises ready for the harvests that were to come.

P. Crampton, memoirs[41]

Right, Albert's Café, Saskatoon, about 1912. This café was founded by Albert Hughes and S. B. Dale, and later owned by Dale. There were, at one time, two or three Albert's Cafés or Restaurants in Saskatoon. These popularly priced restaurants served short orders and full meals, and sold ice cream, cigars, candies, and fruits.

Upper left, McKinley and Mitchell Hardware Store, Biggar, about 1916; Walter Mitchell behind the counter

The Store Clerk's Day
He is expected to present himself at his post at about half past seven in the morning. From that hour until mid-day he is employed variously, in serving customers, in carrying about parcels, bags, boxes, bales, etc. He sweeps out the store, dusts the goods and does anything and everything which his employer deems necessary. . . . At mid-day he is released, dirty and dusty, without any opportunity to enjoy a good breath of fresh air, before he goes to his dinner. Dinner over, a brief lapse of time remains for any rest or recreation ere the short hour is gone. Once more the weary hours drag on until six o'clock finds the footsore clerk trudging out to his supper. . . . At seven o'clock he is still confronted with two and a half hours or more of drudgery. . . .

Saskatoon Phoenix,
2 December 1904

Lower left, bank in Duval, 1913

During the period 1908-11 banks proliferated thruout the province opening up in all sorts of places, even in tents — In 1911 I opened a branch of the Bank in Holdfast using a side room in the Hotel as the Banking office. The safe sent out from Winnipeg was considered to be too heavy for the floor so for the Winter of 1911-12 it stood outside on the platform.

Gordon Bell, letter[42]

Upper right, Northern Electric and Manufacturing Company Limited advertisement, 7 August 1912

In 1911 a neighbour Tom Awde and myself organized the Heward Rural Telephone Company, consisting of fourteen farmer subscribers, we were all on the one line in the country but not in the village. I was president and Tom was the secretary, it was wonderful to be able to talk with thirteen other farmers, especially on urgent matters which did occur sometimes. Our line was merged with other rural lines and later with the main line when extended from Regina with [sic] Heward Village. We had an exchange at the office of J. M. Adams in the village. They had three fine girls who handled it with the assistance of Ruby Reilly occasionally, daughter of Mr. and Mrs. Reilly. A splendid convenience to be able to converse with many in the area with long distance calls anywhere, overcoming the loneliness of early days of homesteading. The natural progress of live settlers.

G. A. Harris, Heward history[43]

Lower right, Maple Creek *News* office, about 1912. Left to right: Les Proud, A. T. White, W. J. Redmond. The *Saskatchewan Herald*, which began publication at Battleford in 1878, was the first newspaper published in what is now Saskatchewan. The importance of a local news media to settlers was indicated by the rapid increase in the number of newspapers published in the newly established towns and villages.

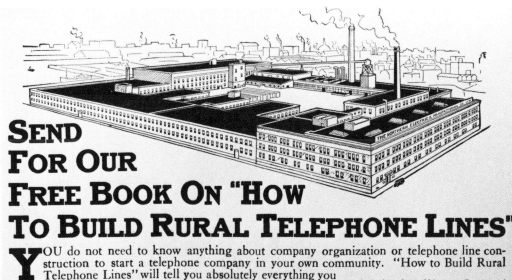

SEND FOR OUR FREE BOOK ON "HOW TO BUILD RURAL TELEPHONE LINES"

YOU do not need to know anything about company organization or telephone line construction to start a telephone company in your own community. "How to Build Rural Telephone Lines" will tell you absolutely everything you need to know. When you have read this book you will be amazed at the simplicity of the whole proposition and wonder why you and your neighbors have not had a telephone system of your own long ago. Sooner or later someone is going to start a telephone system in your neighborhood. Whether you or one of your neighbors chances to be that "someone," you owe it to yourself to be fully informed on the subject.

our book alone shows thirty-seven diagrams and illustrations dealing with this branch of the work. On request we will also tell you of your provincial regulations, what your government demands and what it will do to help you.

Take Free All Our Experience and Knowledge

LET us show you how to get the movement started

Left, city officials watching the laying of mains, Fairford Street West, Moose Jaw, 1904

There were no great speeches or flare of trumpets, but the most important work ever undertaken by the city was inaugurated with a quiet determination to carry it to a successful conclusion.

Moose Jaw Times, *7 July 1904*

Right, Regina cyclone, 30 June 1912: view of the damage caused to residences on Smith Street. Fires, floods, cyclones, and other disasters have been a part of the history of Saskatchewan. Sometimes lives were lost and property damage was high. To growing communities and pioneers struggling to make a living, these events have been catastrophic. One of the most spectacular and devastating disasters to strike Saskatchewan was the Regina cyclone of 1912.

I'll never forget Sunday, June 30, 1912 — the Day of the Cyclone! . . . It was before five when we got back to Mark's home. . . . The atmosphere was very oppressive and the sky filled with black, ominous clouds. . . . Before dinner was far advanced, it started to rain. . . . The rain came down in sheets when suddenly the lights went out and we were unable to see enough to go on with the dinner. . . .

The storm passed quickly, the room became light again and we finished our dinner and then went out onto the verandah. To our surprise, we saw people running along the street. Some appeared to be injured. I heard a woman calling to some neighbors that all the buildings in the park were down. The house we were in had its chimney blown off but received no other serious damage. Myron and I started off to see what had happened but did not have to go far to see some of the effects of the storm . . . only a block or two further . . . [were] rows of buildings lying on the ground completely destroyed and others with lesser damage. . . . we reached Victoria Park . . . buildings around and near the park were hit hard. Three churches had been in the path of the storm: the Baptist, Metropolitan Methodist, and Knox Presbyterian. Each received serious damage but the Metropolitan was a complete wreck. . . . Scores of private houses and other buildings were completely destroyed and 28 people lost their lives. Some of these I knew. . . .

It took Regina a long time to recover from the cyclone. The real estate boom was given a death blow and business fell away seriously. When war broke out in 1914, the effects were still noticeable.

W. T. Moore, memoirs[44]

Upper left, road construction: W. Lovell road gang near Tisdale, about 1908

Lower left, road construction crew south of Redford, 1913

The influx of settlers, whether to the towns or the farms, naturally encouraged the development of industries. For the most part, these were based on resource exploitation or were related to agriculture. There were also a few interesting undertakings which deviated from the expected pattern.

Below, unloading logs, Ladder Lake Company, Camp Seven Landing, about 1920

Very often the load would be four feet above the stakes so the load would be practically twelve feet high. With the stakes spreading at the top the load might be 17 feet wide at the top. This was equivalent to one heavy flat car load. There were four horses as a rule for one sleigh, but on a longer haul we would use six horses and haul a trailer. So those six horses on a heavy load could really haul two flat car loads of logs at once and make two trips a day on a six mile road. . . . The horses would be sharp shod for hauling on the ice road.

Allan Kennedy, reminiscences[45]

Left, coal miners, Estevan, about 1912

Below, Crescent Collieries, Limited, Estevan, 1927

Estevan has been named by some the 'Pittsburgh of Saskatchewan' and it is certainly going along the right lines if it does not quite deserve it yet.... That the Estevan coal is good for steam purposes as well as domestic use there is no gainsaying, as for several years thousands of tons have been shipped to one of the largest manufacturing concerns in Winnipeg, as well as to many smaller manufacturers in other towns in Western Canada.

Regina Leader, *16 December 1911*

Left, drilling a gas well near Maple Creek, about 1908. The Maple Creek Gas, Oil and Coal Company Limited was incorporated in 1907.

Right, Leslie and Wilson Flour Mill, Saskatoon, 1903

Left, brick plant in the Moose Jaw district before 1914

Right, automobile built about 1913 by the Canadian Standard Automobile and Tractor Company, Moose Jaw, with John Robson, who assembled the car, **and** his family, sitting on the running board. The cars were built with parts acquired from the Fort Wayne Engine Company. Very few cars were ever built.

These cars were huge affairs with a wheel base of 132 inches and beautifully built six-cylinder engines with four speed and reverse gear boxes. The bodies had been built for Cadillac and were equally fine. When the first car was finished, it was rolled out and taken up to the race track at the Exhibition Grounds to be tuned up and tested. After some adjustments, the car ran 16 miles on a gallon of gasoline at 45 m.p.h., which was considered fairly good performance. The engine was so smooth and free from vibration that a four-inch lead pencil would stand upright on the radiator cap. Try that with your modern car.

Moose Jaw Times Herald,
5 May 1956

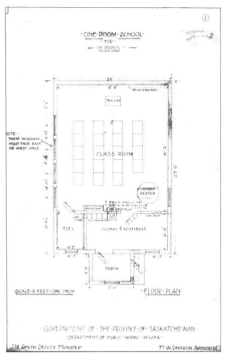

Education was often one of the settler's major concerns. The first school district in the North-West Territories was organized in 1884, after the passing of the School Ordinance in the same year. By 1905, there were 1,190 school districts in Saskatchewan. The recently established Department of Education was in charge of matters pertaining to schools and school districts, although the administration of the district school was the concern of the local ratepayers under a Board of Trustees. Schools, often of log or frame, were constructed by the ratepayers. To aid the local school districts, construction plans outlining proper lighting, heat, and ventilation were supplied by the Department of Education.

Upper left, plan for one-room school, Saskatchewan Department of Public Works, date unknown

Lower left, Coldridge School District No. 242 near Oxbow, about 1905. This one-room school does not appear to have been built according to the accompanying plan, but it is an example of the many schools built in Saskatchewan in the early days.

Right, Eagle Creek School District No. 741, date unknown

The school house, one room, was built on a acre of land with a barn and two out-houses. There was a coal and wood heater for the winter. The janitor would bank the fire at night; that is put large chunks of coal in the heater and close all the drafts. In the morning he would open the drafts and have the room a little warm for school. There was a pail of drinking water with a large enamel dipper that everyone drank from. Often in the winter the water was frozen and it had to be 'unthawed' before we could have a drink.... When recess came she [the teacher] would play ball with us. Other games were Fox and Geese, Pick up Sticks, Nigger Baby, Canny Can, London Bridge and Farmer in the Dell. In summer it was mostly baseball (no soft balls then) and in winter, marbles. What I liked best were the nature hikes. We had many teachers, some good and some not so good.

Josie Olsen Ouellette,
memoirs[46]

Left, school field day, Wroxton, 25 June 1914

While most successful in point of attendance, in the interest shown and in the enjoyment of those competing in the many events comprising the program, the real significance of the first union field day of the public schools of the Wroxton district was in the fact that this, the greatest gathering ever held in this ambitious village, was a gathering of school children of foreign-born parents.

There were upwards of 400 pupils present, every one of them a promising young Canadian. Although their parents were of various nationalities and had come principally from continental Europe, the children gaily waved miniature Union Jacks — the emblem of the freedom their parents have secured for them in their new Canadian home.

Yorkton Enterprise,
25 June 1914

Upper right, Chief Justice F. W. G. Haultain laying the corner-stone for the Regina Normal School, 30 May 1913. In 1893, professional training became compulsory in order to obtain a teacher's certificate. Permanent Normal Schools were established at Regina, Saskatoon, and Moose Jaw.

There is one thing lacking in this country ... I would like to see some way to make the teaching profession a real profession — a profession that a man or a woman can spend his or her life at — giving sufficient returns for the labor and brains demanded, and the time and money spent in preparation for it — carrying with it the honor that attaches to other professions, not the mere unwritten honor of work well done, but something tangible and recognized. I believe that time will come. ...

Chief Justice Haultain,
Regina Leader, *31 May 1913*

Lower right, Sir Wilfrid Laurier laying the corner stone of the College of Agriculture Building, now the Administration Building, University of Saskatchewan, 29 July 1910. An act to establish the University of Saskatchewan was passed by the Legislative Assembly in 1907. Walter C. Murray was appointed as the first president, and in April 1909 Saskatoon was chosen as the site of the university. The first classes in arts and science were offered in the fall of 1909 with an enrollment of seventy students.

Hospitals, located in many of the larger settlements, provided much needed medical services. In 1898, Victoria Hospital was built in Regina. Others followed at Prince Albert, Lloydminster, Battleford, Yorkton, and Moosomin. Many of the hospitals, like the first St. Paul's Hospital in Saskatoon, were private homes converted to serve the public. Provincial health authorities recommended that hospitals be designed to provide sunny, well-ventilated, and fireproof facilities, with room for future expansion.

Upper left, Weyburn General Hospital, about 1913

Lower left, Queen Victoria Cottage Hospital, Yorkton, about 1902

[The Queen Victoria] hospital was opened for patients on the 21st of October, 1902. . . . Its inception was stimulated by, if it was not largely owing to, a contribution of $3,000.00 from the Lady Minto Cottage Hospital Fund, and the hospital is being administered in connection with the Victorian Order by a board of five directors who are elected by the subscribers. It is maintained by voluntary contributions, by fees from patients and by the Government grants. . . . The building itself is a very substantial and attractive one, standing in its own grounds of three acres on an eminence to the southwest of the town. It is on a stone foundation, is built partly of brick and partly of wood, has two stories and a basement, and at present accommodates sixteen patients — public and private. The back half of the second storey is unfinished, and when completed will increase the accommodation to twenty. It has a very good operating room which, for one in use so short a time, is exceedingly well equipped.

Department of Agriculture Annual Report, 1903[47]

Right, building St. Peter's Cathedral, Muenster, 1909

By 1909 the church was becoming too small to accommodate the parishioners and Messrs. August Wassermann and Theodore Fleskes, two carpenters of the parish, were engaged to erect a new church, 56½ x 120 ft. with two 60 ft. towers and a seating capacity of 480. The stone foundation was built by the Bonas Brothers. With many people giving their assistance, it was possible to have the official opening on July 10, 1910....

Berthold Imhoff, a German artist who had opened a studio near St. Walburg, Sask., visited Abbot Bruno and offered to decorate the sancturary of the church with eighty full size figures, gratis. For the body of the church the fee would be $3,000.... on May 12, 1919 he began his work. To commemorate the first Mass on Ascension Day, May 21, 1903, the artist painted a beautiful picture of the Lord's Ascension on the ceiling of the church. He persuaded Abbot Bruno to sit for the portrait.

Muenster history[48]

Left, recreation: outdoor curling at Prince Albert, about 1900-1905

A great revival in the game of curling is in evidence this winter. Several new men, who have until recently withstood the persuasive attractions of the roarin' game are now to be seen on the ice, besom in hand, yelling "soop 'er up," etc. and enjoying themselves to the limit.

Prince Albert Advocate,
24 January 1899

Right, the Fort Qu'Appelle Cycling Club in front of the Hudson's Bay Company Store, Fort Qu'Appelle, 1898; presentation of club colors to the members

A. McDonald, patron of the bicycle club, has presented each member thereof with a handsome set of colors, blue and white, for which he was accorded a hearty vote of thanks. Mr. Robinson took a group photo of the club on Monday p.m., with the H. B. Co's store as a background. The club then formed in line and had their first run to Dr. Seymour's and back, after which Mrs. Smith, vice president, served them with ice cream and cake.

Qu'Appelle Vidette,
15 June 1898

Left, a baseball game in the Qu'Appelle Valley, probably near Lumsden, date unknown. Walter Scott, later premier of Saskatchewan, is believed to be the pitcher.

The large numbers who came from Moose Jaw, Qu'Appelle, Balgonie, Pense, McLean and the settlements of the north found Regina gay and smiling in her holiday dress of bunting, flags and avenues of trees new from the woods but looking as if our streets had always been their natural home. . . .

The day's programme commenced with the

GREAT BASEBALL GAME between Regina and Moose Jaw in the contest for the Hamilton-Tait cup. The play was splendid and both sides were on their mettle. The following was the score, with Regina an inning to spare . . . . [Regina 47, Moose Jaw 24]

Regina Leader, *3 July 1888*

Right, "Hard Time Dance,"
Rosetown, 4 April 1913

The dances usually were very jolly. They were held in a barn. Whole families arrived in sleighs. Babies and small children were made warm and comfortable along one side against the wall, and they slept soundly. Warmth came from a huge stove at one end. Close to it stood the Fiddler and the Caller. The dance always started with a rollicking square dance, the Callers [sic] voice ringing out "Take yer partner, swing her round, over and under, away yer go", and so on. They ended with a waltz to the tune of "Home Sweet Home". Some were danced to a song, thus relieving the Caller. The favourites were "By the Banks of the Saskatchewan" and "The Moon Shines Bright on Red Wing Sighing".

Mrs. W. T. Bibbings, Chaplin[49]

"HARD TIME DANCE" ROSETOWN, APR 4. 1913. Photo by McKenzie

Upper left, Condie Anglican Church Choir, conducted by Thomas Ward, at the First Provincial Music Festival, Regina, May 1909

One thing is very apparent and that is that Saskatchewan possesses musical ability of no mean order and among our cosmopolitan population are many with musical training and ability that would not pass unnoticed in even larger centres and the musical associations are being amply rewarded for their labors in endeavoring to bring this latent talent to the front.... It would almost seem that the keen bracing air of our northern climate must have a beneficial effect on the voices of the rising generation, at least judging by the sweet notes of the youthful singers from Condie who simply brought down the house every time they appeared.

Regina Morning Leader,
15 May 1909

Lower left, Melfort Band at the Tisdale sports day, 1910. The band was led by J. M. Taylor. The members acquired their uniforms in 1909.

Right, music at home, Maple Creek district, 1903. Standing, left to right: Howard Parker, Charlie W. Stearns; seated, left to right: Charlie E. Stearns, Jean Stearns, Jack Stearns

CHAPTER 4

THE MORNING LEADER

PROBS—FAIR AND COOLER. • REGINA, SASK., WEDNESDAY, AUGUST 5, 1914. TODAY'S PAPER 12 PAGES PRICE FIVE CENTS

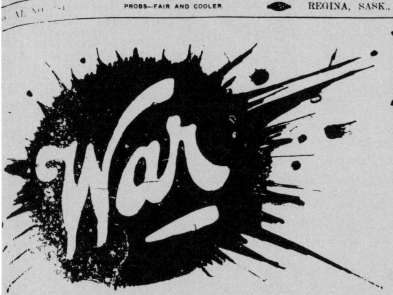

BRITAIN GIVES WORD

GERMANY REJECTED ULTIMATUM OF BRITAIN AS TO BELGIUM AND KING GEORGE DECLARED WAR

ALL EUROPE NOW IN ARMS AUSTRIAN WAR FORGOTTEN IN MOMENTOUS OUTBREAK

UPON THE REQUEST OF BRITAIN AS TO PRESERVA
TION OF NEUTRALITY OF BELGIUM AND BEFORE TIME
OF ULTIMATUM EXPIRED ORDERS FOR CONFLICT
CAME GERMAN FLEET IN NORTH SEA, AND BRITAIN
KNOWS WHERE GRIM COMMENCEMENT MAY BREAK
AT ANY MOMENT

WILL GIVE HOSPITAL SHIP.

TORONTO, Aug. 4—At a meet
ing this afternoon of the executive
of the Imperial Order, Daughters
of the Empire, called to decide
what steps the order should take
in the event of England being
drawn into war, a resolution that
the women of Canada should offer
a hospital ship was unanimously
adopted. The ship will be fully
equipped and placed at the disposal
of the British Admiralty.

SAYS BRITISH HAVE BOTTLED UP FLEET OF GERMAN NAVY

New York Paper Says Kaiser's
Defenders Are Being Held
North of Denmark

HOSTILITIES FLASHES

German Cruisers Active in Al-
giers, and One is Reported
Sunk

KING TO COLONIES

LONDON, Aug. 4. King George
today addressed a message to all
the British colonies expressing his
appreciation of their spontaneous
assurance that they will give the
fullest support to the Motherland.
"They recall to me," His Majesty
says, "the great self sacrifice and
help given by them in the past to
the Mother Country. I shall be
strengthened in the discharge of the
great responsibility which rests on
me that in this trial of the Empire
it will be united, calm and resolute,
and trusting in God."

KAISER EXPLAINS COMING OF WAR WITH RUSSIANS

Tells Parliament How Honor Demanded Strike Against
Russian Duplicity

SIGNAL FLASHED FOR MOST TREMENDOUS NAVAL BATTLE EVER FOUGHT IN HISTOR

LONDON, Aug. 4. England was
immediately after fought King George
to the entire fleet sailing against
action

There conditions were large
glories of the navy. I am sure of
Britain in this hour of trial
Empire.

This was the first message
Plymouth Harbor, and stated to the
Sea. Ever since the wireless has been
to go forth until tonight the signal
battle ever fought spattered up
great naval wireless station.

Immediately after the orders
had been flashed to the admiral
King's own words

NEWS CRIPPLED BY CENSORSHIP

DOMINION PARLIAMENT CALLED

The First World War

In 1914, Saskatchewan citizens greeted the declaration of war with patriotic demonstrations and gave their support to the Allied cause. In addition to men for the armed forces Saskatchewan's chief contribution to the war effort was probably in the production of food. During the war two significant social reforms took place. A measure of prohibition was adopted and women were given the vote. With the return of the veterans and their re-establishment, Saskatchewan turned to a peacetime economy and welcomed a royal visitor.

Left, *Regina Morning Leader*, 5 August 1914

I happened to have been with a great crowd on Hamilton Street when the momentous news was flashed that war was declared against Germany that August 4th day in 1914. Pandemonium broke out, Union Jacks were unfurled and a parade started through the street with wild acclaim "Rule Brittania" and other martial songs were sung. One of the young men I afterwards recruited and examined for the Cameron Highlanders of Winnipeg carried the Union Jack as he sang and paraded. He was afraid the war would be over before he could get there. He did get there but did not get back.

Hugh MacLean, autobiography[50]

Below, "Will You go or Be Sent," *Saskatchewan Herald,* 29 July 1915. During the early years of the war, Canada relied on volunteers for its overseas contingents. Recruiting was a focus of public concern. Newspapers frequently carried general appeals, designed to quicken the sense of duty in prospective volunteers. Saskatchewan's total contribution of men to the overseas forces through the volunteer system and, after 1917, by conscription was approximately 38,000 men.

In the first place it is unquestionably the duty, nay stronger, it is the emphatic duty of every able-bodied, unmarried man to enlist in the army unless prevented by some reason which he can conscientiously give. There are young men who are unmarried but who have responsibilities or obligations which can be given as reasons for not enlisting. But there are thousands of young fellows who only have excuses to offer for not enlisting, and excuses which are manufactured out of whole cloth and convince none but themselves . . . .

A soft snap at home, a best girl, a desire to let others fight your battles for you, these are excuses, and poor ones too, but they are not reasons. Let every unmarried man of able body in Canada ask himself "Am I prevented from enlisting by some reason which I can conscientiously give to my king, my country and myself." Then if the question be honestly asked and answered and the answer be in the negative then their duty is plain.

Saskatchewan Herald, *19 August 1915*

Right, the Twenty-seventh Light Horse under the command of Lieutenant-Colonel George Tuxford leaving Moose Jaw, 23 August 1914

SASKATCHEWAN HERALD

"PROGRESS."

VOL XXXVII.—No. 80   WHOLE NO.—1664   BATTLEFORD, SASK., THURSDAY, JULY 29, 1915 $1.00 PER YEAR

WILL YOU GO OR BE SENT

The Town Engineer Trouble Is Settled at Last by the Council

The regular weekly meeting of the council was held on Monday evening every member being in his seat.

The minutes of the last regular meeting were read and approved.

The following communications were read and disposed of as under:

W. W. Livingston, acknowledging letter with enclosures in the matter of the Lobb & Clark proposition to buy the creamery lots—Filed.

The same, acknowledging instructions with Scottish Tube Co. writ—Finance committee

Wood, Gundy & Co., acknowledging letter re unpaid coupons—Filed.

Terry, Briggs & Slayton, acknowledging wire re coupons falling due—Filed.

The same, telegram enquiring as to probabilities of payment of cou-

Bros be advised that the town would pay their bill as soon as possible; (8) That Ex-Mayor Smith be requested to interview the members of the provincial government while he is in Regina on the subject of the financial situation; (9) That a delegate be sent to Winnipeg to interview the Bank of British North America to endeavor to obtain a line of credit—Adopted.

The police crime report for the week ending July 26 was received and filed.

The constable's report of fees collected included the following clauses That R. H. Speers refused to pay milk vendors' licence as he furnishes milk to the asylum and its employees although some of them reside in the town;   That Cyril Cocks refused to pay poll tax on the ground that he was a rate-

LOCAL NEWS IN BRIEF

The court of revision to hear appeals against the town assessment will be held next Monday afternoon in the council chamber.

A burning chimney on Saturday afternoon caused a fire alarm to be turned in, but before the brigade could turn out, the signal "all out" was sent in.

On Monday two prisoners, H. F. Shoaf and R. Jackson were lodged in the guardroom, having been committed for trial on a charge of housebreaking.

An arrest was made on Monday of a young man who amused himself in driving down 22nd street at a rate considered to be unsafe. He was let go with a caution.

The North Battleford fair takes place on Aug. 9, 10 and 11. The

A Few Gleanings from the Battleford Boys at the Front

J. W. Malloch has received a letter from his sister dated Dumfries, Scotland, under date of July, in which she gives the following particulars of the wounding of "Scotty" Malloch:—

"Possibly you have heard that George was wounded on the 15th of June in France and is now lying in Caird Rest hospital, Dundee. He was fourteen days in France altogether and two days in the trenches when he got his wound by shrapnel. He has had to suffer a great deal owing to the shrapnel still being in his leg. They think they have the most of it out now. He is very thin. He is patient and always in the best of spirits. . . . He is being very well looked after in hospital and the nurses are all very kind to him. He is still in bed and

Mrs. G. G. Smith has received a letter from her husband, giving particulars of his wounding, which occurred on July 4. We are pleased to see from the extract which we have been permitted to make, that Gavin makes light of his injury and we sincerely trust that it is no more serious than he says. The following is an extract:

"I met with an accident the other night and had of course to go to hospital. I was returning with a patrol at night which had been sent out between our trench and the German trench, and in getting over our parapet, which is about seven feet high, I slid down into our trench and came down on a bayonet which went into the fleshy part of my leg just above the knee. The doctor says I will have to keep

Below, St. Chad's Military Hospital, Regina, May 1917. To provide adequate care for soldiers sent home as invalids, the Military Hospitals Commission established a number of convalescent hospitals across Canada. At the request of the commission, a wing of St. Chad's College, an Anglican theological college in Regina, was turned over to the commission in 1916 for use as a hospital. It was used as a convalescent home until the end of the war.

Right, Belgian Relief Fund drive, Regina, date unknown. The Belgian Relief Fund was one of the many war and patriotic funds to which Saskatchewan citizens contributed during the First World War.

Below, Boy Scouts supporting Victory Bond sales, Regina, 1918

Right, "Production and Thrift," *Saskatchewan Farmer*, April 1916. To meet the wartime need for grain to feed a war-ravaged Europe, advertisements such as this were used to obtain a rapid increase in production. Unfortunately such advertisements encouraged the use of some unsound farming practices which may have affected later productivity.

Production and Thrift

GROWING CROPS ON STUBBLE LAND IN 1916

The Empire's Demands for food are greater this year than last.
Less summer-fallow and less fall ploughing than usual in 1915 make
it necessary that the farmers of the Prairie provinces in 1916
shall sow extensively on stubble land

MR. J. H. GRISDALE, Director, and the Superintendents of the Dominion Experimental Farms, urge the following upon the Farmers:

STUBBLE LAND OF FIRST CROP AFTER FALLOW

Burn stubble thoroughly as soon as surface is dry. Fire about noon time when steady wind is blowing. Cultivate at once about two inches deep, then sow the wheat and harrow immediately afterwards. If possible, where area is large, harrow first, then cultivate, seed, and harrow again. In Eastern Saskatchewan sow 1½ bush. per acre; in Western Saskatchewan 1¼ bush. On light soils and dry lands sow ¼ bush. less.

STUBBLE LAND OF SECOND CROP AFTER FALLOW

Usually this land should be summer-fallowed, but this year much of it must be in crop. Burn stubble if possible. This may be helped by scattering straw freely over the field. Wrap old sacking about the end of a 4-foot stick. Dip in gasoline. Set on fire and shake on straw and stubble. Carry gasoline in open pail. If stubble is too light to burn then cultivate, harrow and seed a little lighter than above. Oats and barley will do better than wheat. If shoe drills are used plough instead of cultivating. Plough, pack or roll, and then harrow, if land is grassy or weedy. In the drier sections at least one-third of all cropping land should be summer-fallowed every year.

STUBBLE LAND OF THIRD CROP AFTER FALLOW

Do not sow to grain, but summer-fallow. Better use your spring labour on other stubble land and thus make sure of crops in 1916 and 1917. Put your labour on land that is likely to give best returns.

SEED

Sow only clean, plump seed of tested variety. Use the fanning mill thoroughly and treat seed for smut. Have horses, harness and machines in good shape before starting work.

THE GOVERNMENT OF CANADA

1

THE DEPARTMENT OF AGRICULTURE   THE DEPARTMENT OF FINANCE

In western Canada, one of the social results of the war was the success of a movement for "moral" reform, which centered on the issues of women's suffrage and prohibition. Women in Saskatchewan won the right to vote only after a struggle. The first petition for the vote, signed by 2,500 women, was presented to the Legislature in December 1913. On that occasion Premier Walter Scott expressed the view that the women of Saskatchewan had not shown enough interest. A Provincial Equal Franchise League was organized, and it presented a petition containing 11,000 signatures. When that failed to bring a favorable response, the women organized to get another 10,000 signatures and presented another petition on 14 February 1916. This time they were successful.

Left, from the *Grain Growers' Guide*, 26 February 1913

Right, from the *Regina Morning Leader*, 15 February 1916

SPEAK!

VOTES FOR WOMEN

At the last session of the Saskatchewan Legislature Premier Scott expressed himself as in favor of extending the franchise to women, but did not care to enact the necessary legislation until the women of Saskatchewan asked for it. It is now up to the women to "SPEAK" in clear and unmistakable terms.

WOMEN RECEIVE THE VOTE FROM SCOTT GOVERNMENT AT MEMORABLE ST. VALENTINE'S DAY ASSEMBLY

Petitions and Addresses Rewarded Promptly and Decisively

"THIS IS SO SUDDEN, SIR"

President of Provincial Equal Franchise Board Voices Thanks of Workers

Yesterday was a great day for the women of Saskatchewan. Before an audience of many women, drawn from all parts of the province and representing all the women of Saskatchewan, Hon. Walter Scott, premier of Saskatchewan, in the Legislative Assembly hall at the Parliament Buildings, gave the women the franchise and placed every adult in this province on the same footing.

It was the end of one phase of the struggle of women to be recognized as the equal of man in the matter of the franchise. It marked the opening of bigger responsibilities, greater tasks, the struggle for the victory of the highest ideals in the home and in the state.

le, but very alert woman who is at the head of the Provincial Equal Suffrage board, having addressed the premier and the house, said: "Our deputation waits upon you today to urge you to grant us equal franchise rights with men. When we last petitioned for the ballot, 10,000 names strong, we went away somewhat disappointed, but not cast down. We went to work again to continue our educative movement, and later when more petitioning was asked of us, we shouldered that, too. We have prepared a map which shows at a glance how much of the province has been canvassed.

"Mr. Premier, we have reason to be grateful to you for much of the recent legislation you have enacted. Already many have benefitted by the Homestead Act and have felt the value of its protection. Your temperance legislation we have followed closely. Today we ask for the women of the province the chance to register their votes with the men's.

"The Municipal vote has been used by the women in such manner that you need have no fear but they will use the wider privilege to good advantage. In my own town of Yorkton, 58 per cent. of the women eligible made use of their vote, compared with 40 per cent. of the men eligible. I had feared an unusual number of spoiled ballots, but the percentage was lighter than the previous year. Had it been the reverse, the women

In response to temperance demands and partly as a war measure, bars in Saskatchewan were closed as of 1 July 1915. All bar and club licenses were abolished, and liquor was only available through government liquor stores for off-premises consumption. In 1917 the stores were closed, and liquor could only be bought in drugstores on prescription. Drinking elsewhere than in a private home was prohibited. Provision for the sale of beer by the glass in licensed premises was not made until 1935.

Upper right, bar in the Windsor Hotel, Saskatoon, 1903

Lower right, from the *Grain Growers' Guide*, 26 May 1915

The closing of the bars has resulted in untold good to many throughout the district. Business men, doctors, storekeepers and farmers all agree that it was a long step in the right direction. From a police point of view the decrease of petty crimes was soon noticeable, the change being most marked here in Moosejaw, [sic] where we handle all prisoners convicted and sentenced to jail. The number so handled during the past year has decreased 75 per cent.

J. A. McGibbon, Superintendent, Royal North-West Mounted Police, report, 1917[51]

The Kerrobert Citizen

KERROBERT, SASK., THURSDAY, NOVEMBER 14th, 1918.

THE WAR IS WON

Germany Accepts the Armistice Terms of the Allies

PEACE IS AT HAND

RIGHT IS VICTORIOUS - DEMOCRACY IS CROWNED

THE ARMISTICE WAS SIGNED BY GERMANY AT 12 A.M. MONDAY MORNING, PARIS TIME.   THE NEWS
WAS RECEIVED IN KERROBERT AT 3   A.M. MONDAY MORNING, KERROBERT TIME.

BUY VICTORY BONDS AND BRING THE BOYS HOME. YOU WANT TO SEE THEM, THEY WANT TO SEE YOU.

DO NOT BE ASHAMED OF THE PART YOU HAVE PLAYED WHEN YOU MEET THEM FACE TO FACE ONCE MORE

We Remember Today The Boys Who Can Never Return

Sergeant Graham
Kelfield

Lce. Cpl. W. M. Sample

Cpl. Cave and
Lieut. Tripp

Below, parade of returned veterans, Biggar, 1919

Left, "Denied Access to the Land which He Bled to Defend," 6 March 1918. The Soldier Settlement Act of 1917 made provision for veterans who wished to farm to draw loans of $2,500 for the purchase of livestock and equipment and to homestead under existing regulations. Applications for soldier entries exceeded expectations, and there were justifiable complaints that some of the lands which should have been available for returned soldiers were being held vacant by speculators. The Soldier Settlement Act of 1919 subsequently authorized that these lands be purchased by the Soldier Settlement Board and made available to veterans.

Grain Growers' Guide
March 6, 1918

The visit of the Prince of Wales to Canada in 1919 symbolized a return to normal times following the war. The main purpose of the tour appears to have been to renew the bonds of empire. The Prince's visit to over fifty Canadian towns and cities endeared him to Canadians throughout the Dominion.

Below, His Royal Highness The Prince of Wales at a stampede at Saskatoon, 11 September 1919

The crowning moment of the day came when he requested permission at the stampede to ride a broncho. When he climbed out of the royal pavilion to the back of the horse and rode up the track in front of the grandstand, the last bonds of restraint broke, and the entire gigantic attendance rose to their feet ... his face fairly beamed, and another terrific burst of applause followed as he lined his horse up in the centre of a ring of cowboys and had his picture taken. That the Prince enjoyed this ... was plain by his joyous smile.

Saskatoon Phoenix, *12 September 1919*

CHAPTER 5

A Time of Change and Hope

The decade of the twenties, coming as it does between the First World War and the Great Depression, is often overlooked, but much happened in Saskatchewan during that period. While the provincial Liberal party retained power for most of the twenties, it was a time of considerable political uncertainty and change, as attempts were made to resolve western problems. Farms became more mechanized, and farmers organized co-operatives to help market their grain and other products. Towns and cities grew and became more attractive with electricity, running water, radios, motion picture theaters, and other social and cultural amenities. The increasing use of the automobile and truck created a need for better roads and bridges. Airplanes, although still somewhat a novelty, began to appear in Saskatchewan's sky. The boundary of development was extended northward, and there was a renewal of immigration. The diverse ethnic composition of the population gave rise to religious and racial prejudices which reached their most widespread expression when the Ku Klux Klan operated in Saskatchewan. In the 1929 provincial election, the Liberal party was defeated for the first time since 1905 and replaced by a Co-operative Government made up of Conservatives, Progressives, and Independents. As the decade ended Saskatchewan began to feel the effects of the growing, worldwide depression.

The entrance of the Progressives into federal and provincial politics during the 1920s was the result of disenchantment with the "old-line" parties and caused a breakdown of the two-party system which had previously existed in Saskatchewan. These were years of political change and confusion during which independent candidates, under a variety of names and supporting a variety of platforms, were nominated in many provincial constituencies to oppose not only Liberal and Conservative candidates but also one another.

Left, Progressives on the road to victory, Moose Jaw, 1923. E. N. Hopkins, sitting in the buggy, was elected member of Parliament for Moose Jaw in the by-election of 10 April 1923.

The importance of agricultural production had been underlined during the war and in the years that followed, bringing a challenge of improvement to the grain frontier. Farming meant more than the application of labor to land. Research aimed at the improvement of seed grains and agricultural methods, and the use of more sophisticated machinery began to change Saskatchewan agriculture. Farm production and the marketing and transporting of agricultural produce underwent significant changes as the twenties progressed.

Below, from the *Grain Growers' Guide*, 12 January 1921. A more orderly system for the marketing of grain, under which farmers would not be at the mercy of fluctuating prices on the grain exchange and the vagaries of the railway system had always been a goal of the organized farmers. When the operation of the Canadian Wheat Board, established as a war measure, was terminated in 1920, farmers' organizations requested that it be reinstated. When this was not done, they turned to wheat pools to solve their problems.

Clearing the Right of Way

Right, Aaron Sapiro, 1927. The Saskatchewan Grain Growers' Association and the Farmers' Union of Canada invited Aaron Sapiro, an expert in co-operative marketing from California, to Saskatchewan. In August 1923, he addressed large meetings in Saskatoon, Regina, Moose Jaw, and Swift Current on the idea of a contract wheat pool. By June 1924, a Saskatchewan Wheat Pool was an accomplished fact. Sapiro not only raised the farmers' enthusiasm for a wheat pool but stressed the need for a unification of the two farm organizations. This was achieved in 1926 when the United Farmers of Canada (Saskatchewan Section) was formed as a result of the merger. Sapiro frequently returned to Saskatchewan to publicize the advantages of co-operative marketing.

Below, Saskatchewan Wheat Pool information tent, Weyburn fair, 1927

Right, entrance to the Sherwood Building, Regina, about 1926

"The entrance doors to the Sherwood Building, Regina are very remarkable," states Mr. W. Waldron, Saskatchewan Markets Commissioner. *"The various names emblazoned thereon in gold letters indicate that here the Saskatchewan Wheat Pool, the Saskatchewan Poultry Pool, The Saskatchewan Live Stock Pool and The Saskatchewan Dairy*

Pool have their headquarters as well as the Saskatchewan Pool Elevators and the Saskatchewan Grain Growers' Association . . . This doorway might well be termed the 'Escutcheon of the Pools' representing as it does agricultural co-operative development in the province. No fewer than 75,000 farmers have a joint interest in the business carried on behind these doors, and millions of dollars are mailed from these offices in the course of a year by way of payment to members for the farm produce marketed for them by their own organisations.

Public Service report, 1926[52]

Left, Seager Wheeler, 1869-1961, came to Canada in 1885 and in 1887 bought a farm near Rosthern. A breeder of hard spring wheat he developed Kitchener and Red Bobs, and, from the latter, Early Triumph and Supreme. Between 1911 and 1918 he won five world wheat championships and many awards for other field crops.

To Mr. Wheeler belongs the distinction of being the world's champion wheat breeder, gaining that title by capturing the thousand-dollar prize at the recent New York exhibition .... the competition was keenly contested by all the most prominent grain growers of North America and the winning of it by a Saskatchewan farmer is one of the biggest advertisements of our soil for wheat-growing purposes that the province could possibly have.

Regina Leader,
22 November 1911

Upper right, Better Farming Train, date unknown

In June and July of 1915 to 1918 the College of Agriculture participated in a unique and colorful means of carrying agricultural information to farming communities throughout the province. This was the Better Farming Train. In 1915 it consisted of eighteen cars and coaches including a well-appointed diner and sleeping coach. One coach was equipped for the care of young children while their parents visited the train. Three coaches were converted to lecture cars, one of which was devoted to lectures and demonstrations in household science. The other flat cars and coaches carried exhibits of live-stock, field crops, farm machinery, poultry and dairying. For six weeks the train made three stops each day — forenoon, afternoon and evening. Thousands of men, women and children visited the train, many coming long distances by buggy and wagon, sometimes forty or fifty miles.

Lawrence E. Kirk, College of Agriculture history[53]

Lower right, Field Day at the farm of Charles Marks, Midale, 4 July 1922

A new feature was tried out this year, viz. that of holding a picnic or field day at the home of a farmer who had made good in some one or more lines of endeavor, such as crop or live stock production. One was held on the farm of Charles Marks at Midale. Mr. Marks has the only silo in his district and a herd of good Holstein cows, quite a large acreage of corn, sunflowers and sweet clover. What Mr. Marks had done was used by the speakers present from the College and the Department to show others what might be done to improve agriculture. An automobile tour was arranged in the Snipe Lake district and a number of good farms were visited to the end that suggestions might be found that would lead to improvement in farm practice.

Dean of Agriculture, report for 1922[54]

Below, Professor R.D. Ramsay, Department of Extension, University of Saskatchewan, demonstrating sheep judging, Melfort Farm Boys' Camp, Melfort Fair, 1928. Farm Boys' Camps were conducted by the agricultural societies with financial assistance provided by the provincial and federal governments. The Department of Extension, University of Saskatchewan provided staff for the program.

Right, Farm Girls' Week at the University of Saskatchewan, June 1935. The instructor was Miss Edith C. Rowles, Assistant, Department of Household Science. The courses were organized by the Department of Extension, University of Saskatchewan.

Thirty-two eager, interested girls from 18 to 23 years of age gathered at

the University of Saskatchewan, June 25 to 28, for a course in community leadership embracing domestic and leisure time activities . . . . the girls took part in home canning demonstrations, in amateur dramatics and in handicraft diversions. The artistic effects and the pleasure to be obtained from such work as rug-making, petit point, etc. proved to the girls that these arts are truly cultural and not merely methods of combatting hard times. . . .

Sealers, spoons and wash boilers took on a new significance when Farm Girls gathered at the domestic science laboratory . . . where they undertook a short course in home canning under the able direction of Miss Edith Rowles . . . . some of the girls prepared and canned tomatoes. . . . Others canned strawberries or spinach, turning out a delightful assortment of sealers. . . . Western Producer, *11 July 1935*

Farm Girls at University of Sask, Saskatoon, June, 1935.

Gibson Photo

The development of educational extension programs was neither the only nor the most significant innovation to affect agriculture during the twenties. Advances in farm machinery gradually changed the nature of farm operations, though for many years the old way coexisted with the new.

Left, Nova Scotia stookers, Maxwell farm, 1924

Harvesters are pouring into the west at the rate of 500 or 600 a day. Special trains are bringing them to distributing points, such as Regina and Moose Jaw, and from these points, the harvesters are shifting for themselves....

A special C.N.R. train carrying 550 left Winnipeg last night and will arrive in Regina today....

A C.P.R. special train carrying about 600 arrived in the city last night bound for Moose Jaw, where the train will be broken up, and the harvesters distributed to the south, west and north.

Regina Morning Leader, *21 August 1924*

Below, harvesting on the farm of Joseph Embree, St. Boswells, 1929

One of the oustanding benefits of the combine method of harvesting is the amount of help in harvest time. On my farm here, consisting of a section and a half, three men harvested the 1928 crop. Myself on the combine, one man on the tractor and one on the grain truck. This was our harvest crew, compared with from four to seven men when threshing with a separator. The biggest problem in my estimation, ... is the ripening of the grain.... Nevertheless, the combine and truck method is so far ahead of binder, stooking and threshing, that if the cost was the same for both methods I would prefer the combine by far, with its efficiency and small handling crew.

Western Producer, *27 June 1929*

Left, hauling grain to the elevator at Norquay, June 1920

Right, hauling bales with an International truck, date unknown

Last fall I started drawing grain with a truck and had a man drawing with one team . . . . As a general rule I had [the] fifth load unloaded and got home ahead of him after his second load . . . . This, of course, is not the only work I do with my truck. It would be impossible to make a list of all the trips I have made and what I went after, but they range all the way from going to town for a few groceries to [sic] about three thousand pounds of live hogs . . . . The closest truck to me is pretty close to twelve miles away in one direction and I don't know how far you have to go in the other three directions to find trucks . . . .

Anonymous[55]

Agriculture was not the only industry in Saskatchewan to be affected by new technology during the twenties. Though some jobs continued to be done as they had been for decades, many others were made less laborious by the introduction of improved machinery.

Upper left, fishermen leaving Big River for Peter Pond Lake with their winter outfit, 1927

Commercial fishing has been carried on for about 10 years in spite of the serious handicap of the long transportation to the railways and usually a long railway shipment to the market. Fish from this district are sent as far east as Chicago and Montreal and south to St. Paul and neighboring points. It has only been possible to carry on the industry during the winter when they could be handled from the lakes to the railway in a frozen condition. . . .

The output here . . . during the winter of 1919 reached a total of three and half million pounds, shipped through Big River. . . . The lakes fished in during that winter were Doré Lake, which supplied over half, McBeth channel and Churchill Lake, of next importance, and the smaller lakes such as Keely, Delaronde and la Plonge. The fish shipped by way of the Great Waterways railway were caught in Peter Pond lake. It can be seen therefore that some of the most important lakes were scarcely touched.

S.D. Fawcett, report, 1920[56]

Lower left, setting a muskrat trap, 1908

If the water is steady, not fluctuating in height, I'd come along on my raft, and just make a little hollow in the bank, big enough to hold my trap, set my trap there in about an inch or two of water and stick a piece of any kind of vegetable on a little stick and put it back into the hole. That worked good — the muskrats would see that or smell it.

Ted Updike, interview[57]

Upper right, lumberjacks at Frederick's Camp, Mistatim, about the 1920s

Lower right, steam hauler, the Pas Lumber Company Limited, Carrot River, about the 1920s

Below, construction of the Island Falls Power Development on the Churchill River, July 1929

The Island Falls power plant on the Churchill river commenced operating about a month ago, and marks the first commercial development of water power in Saskatchewan. The initial installation consists of three 14,000 h.p. units, and provision has been made for three additional units, on completion of which the station will have a capacity of 86,500 h.p.

. . . It was constructed by the Churchill River Power Company, a wholly-owned subsidiary of the Hudson Bay Mining & Smelting Company, principally for the purpose of providing power for the operation of the Flin Flon mine and smelter. . . . Under an agreement with the government of Saskatchewan, one sixth of the power developed is reserved for the use of the province.

"Saskatchewan's First Hydro Plant," August 1930[58]

Right, harvesting anhydrous cake at the sodium sulphate deposit, Alsask, September 1929

Though the production and refining of sodium sulphate is one of the newest 'mining' industries in Saskatchewan, it has attained an enviable position, ranking second only to coal in importance, notwithstanding that market demands have been quite irregular. . . . More than two hundred alkali deposits have been found in Saskatchewan. . . . The present operating dehydration plants are at Dunkirk, Ormiston, Alsask, Fusilier, and White Shore Lake.

Magazine article, May 1935[59]

Upper left, assembling graders, Richardson Road Machinery, Saskatoon, 1931

Lower left, a sash-and-door factory, North Battleford, no date

Right, Urban development: Leask during the 1920s

Left, Hotel Saskatchewan, a Canadian Pacific hotel under construction, Regina

An army of 1,000 workmen, representing almost 40 trades and separate phases of work, took part in the construction of the Hotel Saskatchewan from the first start on the removal of buildings from the site until the hotel was ready to receive the public. . . . Every morning for almost a month this army arrived at the half-built building and worked with energy until nightfall. Then started the night-shift, carrying on until dawn.

During the last few weeks many women were employed in preparing the rooms, making beds and putting the finishing touches to the dressers and dusting the rooms and furniture.

Regina Leader, *23 May 1927*

Right, a busy scene on Saskatoon's Second Avenue, probably late 1920s

Owing to the advantages derived from its central location and railway facilities, Saskatoon has already become the second largest distributing point in Western Canada. . . . It serves an area of over 45,000 square miles, having more than 200 thriving towns and villages on 1686 miles of operating lines. . . . The business portion of the city is built of brick, stone and concrete. Excellent building stone is quarried within a short distance.

E. Breed, Saskatoon[60]

Left, Fort Qu'Appelle Sanatorium built by the Saskatchewan Anti-Tuberculosis League, 1918. By 1922 the "insidious and deadly menace" of tuberculosis was so serious that in co-operation with the Saskatchewan Anti-Tuberculosis League the provincial government undertook to build two new sanatoriums to provide the necessary treatment centers.

Small T.B. Associations were formed throughout the Province for the purpose of educating the people on the subject and to raise funds for the building of a sanatorium. This was followed in 1911 by the formation of a Provincial Anti-T.B. League with Peter McAra of Regina as President. This was a voluntary organization which raised $97,000.00 by public subscription as a start for the building of the first San at Fort Qu'Appelle. This unit was opened in October, 1917, and accommodated sixty

patients. Fortunately, the first superintendent was Dr. George Ferguson, who, over the years, became a world renowned figure and became one of the world's leaders in the treatment of tuberculosis. At the outset, the Provincial Government took no part in financing this building but did allow the standard hospital grant of 50¢ a day.... This Anti-T.B. League did a wonderful job.

Hugh MacLean, autobiography[61]

Below, laying the cornerstone for the Weyburn Mental Hospital, 19 May 1921. The building of the Weyburn Mental Hospital was a part of the development of medical services in Saskatchewan. The hospital, constructed to accommodate 400 patients, had special quarters for tubercular patients. It was built at a cost of $2 million.

Upper left, Saskatchewan Provincial Police officers, Moose Jaw detachment, 1926. Left to right: A. Band, R. Pyne, S. Kistruck, A. Cassidy. Social change in urban and rural Saskatchewan increased the need for law enforcement. In 1917, the Saskatchewan Provincial Police force was organized to take over the provincial duties of the Royal Canadian North-West Mounted Police. The provincial police continued to police the province until May 1928 when they were disbanded.

Far left, below, Saskatchewan Provincial Police patrol boat, Nipawin, 1921

Left, below, Regina's first motorcycle policeman, Dalton W. Fisher, with his Harley-Davidson, about 1930

Upper right, Constable Martin McDonald, Saskatoon City Policeman with an early police vehicle, late 1920s

Lower right, Royal Canadian Mounted Police, Carlyle detachment, with a still seized in the Moose Mountains north of Arcola, 1938; Corporal R. S. Pyne (left) and Corporal M. F. Lindsay

Left, transportation: Aerial Service Company Limited, Regina, 1920; R. J. Groome, president. The hangar was located two blocks south of the Legislative Building and four blocks west of Albert Street.

Regina has the honor of having the first airplane registered in Canada, the first commercial pilot's license and the first air engineer's license and the first registered air harbor, or airdrome, in Canada.

Regina Morning Leader, *21 April 1920*

Below, Royal Canadian Air Force base at Ladder Lake near Big River, August 1929. The aircraft in the picture include Vedettes, Vikings, and Vancouver flying boats built by Canadian Vickers. Forest-fire suppression flights were made from this base from 1925 to about 1935.

The most important single development in forest fire protection in late years has been in the use of aircraft for the detection and suppression of incipient forest fires, constituting a measure of prevention rather than a cure. Where lakes are numerous flying boats can be used both for detection and for the transportation of fire-fighters and their equipment to fires in remote areas. Where safe landing places are few, land [based] machines are used for the detection and inspection of fires only. The aircraft are equipped with wireless and can report the exact location of a fire as soon as it has been detected. These aircraft can be used incidentally for exploring remote areas and mapping them by means of aerial photography.

Canada Year Book, *1929*

Upper left, the Batoche Ferry, 1923. For many years ferries were the chief means of crossing rivers in Saskatchewan. In 1920 there were forty-three ferries in operation but their numbers have declined as many have been replaced by bridges. Since 1912 ferries have been free except for a night toll fee.

Lower left, the Nipawin Bridge, about the 1940s

An arrangement was entered into with the Canadian Pacific Company to obtain a highway crossing on the bridge they are constructing over the Saskatchewan River at Nipawin. Plans call for a double decked bridge with highway floor beneath the railway.

The work is being carried out by the railway company, the department [of highways] paying a percentage of the cost based on the extra amount of labour and material required for the combined bridge. The work started in the summer of 1928, and good progress has been made, and it is expected the bridge will be in commission by the spring of 1930.

Department of Highways annual report, 1929[62]

Right, David Bare, Imperial Oil agent, Moose Jaw, 1921. With the growing use of the automobile and truck, the ubiquitous service station became a feature of streets and highways.

Upper left, street maintenance: dragging a Prince Albert street, date unknown

Maintenance is something that we have with us always, and few of us realize its importance. . . . Keeping the ditches and culverts clean, cutting weeds and brush from the right-of-way and keeping the surface of the road free from ruts or other irregularities are the most apparent features of maintenance. . . . The frequent use of a road drag tends to produce undulations in the road surface, and it is now generally recognized that a small blade grader is a much more efficient tool for maintenance work.

Maintenance is the key to the earth road situation.

R. H. MacKenzie, address[63]

Lower left, road conditions: main street of Blaine Lake, about the 1930s

Motorists returning to the city from all directions reported the roads to be in terrible condition . . . a great many car owners were leaving their cars wherever they happened to be and were returning to the city by train. . . . A farmer at one place on the road was pulling out cars so fast as they came along . . . a few places between Hague and Saskatoon were reported to be 'not so good' but with chains it was possible to get through.

Saskatoon Phoenix,
3 July 1928

Right, clearing snow from the rail line near Victoria Plains, 1947. Keeping the rail lines open in the winter time has often proved to be a problem in Saskatchewan and has made winter travel, even by railway, somewhat uncertain.

From the cupola I obtained a good view of the advance engine at work. It was marvellous to see her rush at full speed into a drift, disappear in the cloud of flying snow, and re-appear on the other side, leaving a clear tunnel behind. On one of these occasions she did not reappear and when the snow settled she was in the centre of the drift and black smoke was issuing from her smokestack. Our train moved forward to the edge of the drift and the shovellers, thirty-one in number, swarmed into the cut and the work of digging her out commenced.

Moose Jaw Times,
28 April 1893[64]

If the twenties began to put a new face on Saskatchewan's physical and commercial development, they also brought some new ideas about ways of having fun. At the same time, people made the most of entertainments which had been devised in earlier years. The twenties, after all, are often remembered as a decade of gaiety and good times.

Below, Prince Albert Exhibition, 1917

A big ferris wheel is numbered among the attractions, and while riding in it, one may secure an excellent view. Something entirely new is provided, however, in the Frolic, a riding device which was only given to the American public this year. It is certainly the very latest and the motion duplicates the waves of the sea.

Prince Albert Daily Herald
10 August 1917

Upper right, children advertising a Chautauqua in Prince Albert, date unknown. Chautauqua, a traveling cultural show, brightened local life in Saskatchewan. Its entertainment and educational program, which continued for several days, often included music, drama, and lectures. People of all ages looked forward to this annual event. The depression and the development of entertainment media in the 1930s brought an end to chautauqua tours.

Lower right, a view of the Chautauqua held at Manitou Lake, 1922

Thursday 22 [June 1922]
. . . Chautauqua in afternoon. Lecture "The Homing of the People," Lethe Coleman. Evening "Other Peoples [sic] Money." Home at 12.
Friday 23
. . . At Chautauqua afternoon and evening concert . . . Lecture "Why or the Problem of Life," Matheson Wilbur Chase.
Saturday 24
. . . At Chautauqua in evening. Lecture "The Wonders of Electricity." A masterly exposition.
Sunday 25
. . . At service in the Chautauqua tent. Rev. Archibald Recker Preacher. "The Four Horsemen of the Apocalypse."

William Good, diary[65]

Left, fire curtain in the Biggar theater. The scene was painted by a local artist, and the advertisements were paid for by local merchants.

Upper right, local drama group, Biggar, about 1922

Lower right, Shellbrook movie theater. Theater, vaudeville, silent films, and talkies found their place in the lighter side of Saskatchewan life. Safety standards for the buildings and movie projectors were as much a public concern as was the moral influence of the entertainment.

Left, poolroom, Wakaw, 1921

At present there are no provincial regulations for poolrooms, billiard rooms, bowling alleys etc. . . . and these places run at their own sweet will as to hours of closing, and as to youths frequenting them. . . . As I go through the Province I hear many complaints about the evil influences of some of the poolrooms, both as resorts for late gambling, and as unwholesome resorts for youth. . . .

Rev. W. P. Reekie,
letter, 1922[66]

Right, a family picnic, 1924

Left, Kathleen Flannigan in the South Saskatchewan River, Saskatoon, 1925

Today if a girl or a woman wishes to experience the thrill of a high dive and a long swim, there is no mock modesty sponsored by restricting conventions that compels her to risk her life in a cumbersome bathing costume, such as the American woman of earlier generations was forced to wear.

Instead she steps forward on the spring board clad in a comfortable highly practical, close fitting suit of knitted jersy that permits the bodily freedom necessary if one is to be a good strong swimmer. . . .

Prince Albert Daily Herald,
16 June 1923

Right, swimming in the White Mud River near Eastend, 1921

Left, Grey Owl meeting a party of tourists at Beaver Lodge, Ajawaan Lake, Prince Albert National Park, 1932. The park was officially opened on 10 August 1928.

He worked for the protection of the forests and a means of educating people in order to prevent the damage of forests by fires. He wished to devise ways and means of capturing fur-bearing animals without unnecessary cruelty. He fought against the cruelty of blood sports so that animals should have a fair chance for their life. ... In all these objectives Grey Owl had done a great work....

Regina Leader-Post,
25 April 1938

Right, motor campground, Waskesiu Lake, Prince Albert National Park, 1937

Left, Frank and Jim Bentley listening to a five-tube Westinghouse radio, 1926

. . . in the fall [of 1927] we got our first radio, it was a Westinghouse, a huge thing that took two C batteries, 3 B's and a wet cell battery, like a car's. The B's and C's were big, so we had to buy a library table to put the radio on, and put a shelf underneath to put the batteries on. We already had the phone in the house by 1922, so we figured we were living in the lap of luxury when we got the car and a radio, which were almost the first in the district. The radios in those days were very temperamental, sometimes all you would get was squeals. Ours though, was usually good. . . .

Alice Light, memoirs[67]

Right, travelling library at a farm house, about 1945

In eleven years the number of travelling libraries in the province has increased from the original Box No. 1 sent out in 1914, to more than eleven hundred libraries, and yearly circulation of the books has gradually increased from a few hundred to considerably over half a million. . . . It is quite impossible to meet all the requests . . . but no legitimate appeal for books ever goes unheeded, and if a library cannot be sent at the time bundles of old books are sent. Bundles of old books are also sent to small isolated communities of three or four families, who are anxious for books, but haven't enough people in the district to justify the sending of a library and occasionally the men in a construction or a lumber camp get a lot of pleasure out of a huge box of worn travelling library books.

Public Service report, 1925[68]

Libraries and other community services which developed during the twenties were generally intended for use by everyone, regardless of religious or national background. Still, the people of Saskatchewan remained conscious of ethnic differences throughout the twenties.

Upper left, Rudolph Fester family, St. Walburg, 1929. These German immigrants arrived from Poland in June 1929.

Lower left, Galician farm near Wakaw, 1921

Below, pioneer celebration at Hryhoriw, 3 October 1937. The Hryhoriw school district was located near Buchanan.

. . . Immigrants came to Canada from many countries. Their coming in many cases was not due to encouragement offered by the department [of immigration]. From war-torn Europe numbers came to escape the poverty, wretchedness and national unrest that followed the Great War. The pressure of conditions at home, coupled with the persuasion of relatives or friends in Canada, are the underlying causes of not a small part of the present-day movement towards Canada from several countries of Europe.

Canada, Sessional Papers, 1925[69]

Left, a Russian family on a farm near Lorenzo, northwest of Blaine Lake, 1922

Right, an Indian family at the mouth of the Foster River, 1926

INVISIBLE EMPIRE

KNIGHTS of the KU KLUX KLAN

Dear Sir:—

This is a personal invitation to you for admission in attending a meeting of the Invisible Empire, Knights of the Ku Klux Klan to be held in the *Orange Temple* on *Tuesday Nov 27* at 8 p.m. sharp.

This invitation is sent to you as a direct desire of one of your friends who is interested in this great movement of today and has intimated to the local committee your probable interest.

You are neither implicated nor under any obligation in attending but come only as a free citizen of your own free will to hear a stirring expose of certain conditions based upon the rights relative to the principles set forth on this page, one of our educational lectures.

PRINCIPLES OF THIS MOVEMENT

PROTESTANTISM	RESTRICTIVE AND SELECTIVE IMMIGRATION
RACIAL PURITY	FREEDOM OF SPEECH AND PRESS
GENTILE ECONOMIC FREEDOM	LAW AND ORDER
JUST LAWS AND LIBERTY	HIGHER MORAL STANDARD
SEPARATION OF CHURCH AND STATE	ONE PUBLIC SCHOOL
PURE PATRIOTISM	FREEDOM FROM MOB VIOLENCE

PLEASE PRESENT THIS INVITATION AT THE MEETING

Left, invitation to a meeting of the Invisible Empire Knights of the Ku Klux Klan, 1928. The Klan was an important factor in the highly emotional provincial election campaign of 1929.

Right, Courval School District, No. 2710, no date — an indication of the religious prejudice which was in evidence during the 1920s.

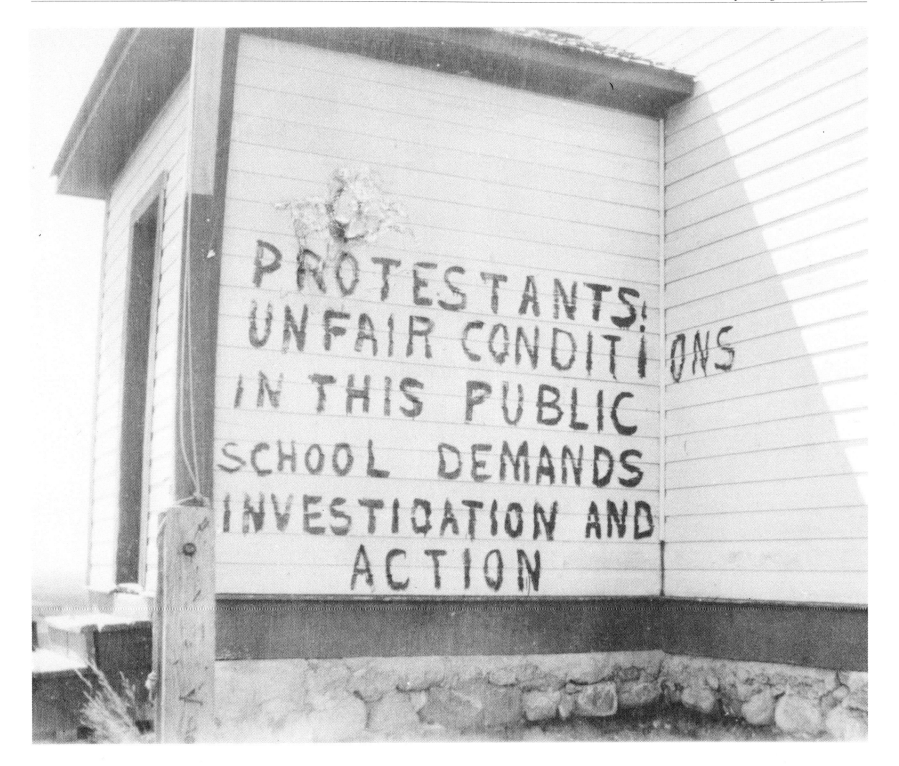

CHAPTER 6

Hope Deferred

Drifting soil and abandoned farms became an all-too-familiar sight in southern Saskatchewan as a result of the drought of the thirties. Coincident with the drought was a worldwide depression which created widespread unemployment and a drastic fall in prices for agricultural products. It was a time of severe economic difficulty that placed a heavy burden on governments to provide relief for those unable to provide the necessities of life for themselves. By the time the decade of the thirties ended there had been severe social and economic dislocations, and political changes had occurred in the province.

Left, an abandoned farm near Estevan, 1939

Well, I remember when the first dirt storms hit us. It was dead still outside and we wondered if it was a tornado or something that was coming, the sky was so black and we just stood outside and watched it and the air was just still and then it hit us. We had to hold pillows at the windows to keep them from breaking. It was just like a sheet of black; it was just dirt; it came from the west and from then on we had terrific dirt storms. Nothing grew, not even the weeds on the summerfallow which is something.

Edna Staples McIntosh, interview[70]

In 1931, tension between coal miners and mine owners in the Estevan area reached a breaking point. The roots of the trouble lay in the seasonal nature of the coal work, low wages, and poor working and living conditions. Actual conflict was triggered by the economic dislocations of a mounting depression. A month-long strike among the mineworkers culminated in a tragic clash, known as "Black Tuesday," which resulted in three deaths and numerous injuries sustained by strikers, police, and bystanders.

Below, Estevan Riot, 29 September 1931: street scene during the riot

Police and striking miners clashed on the streets of Estevan today when the authorities attempted to prevent miners ... from entering the town and parading.

The miners ... proceeded to Estevan with the avowed intention of going to the town hall, where their meeting had been forbidden .... When within a block of the town hall, the miners were met by a cordon of police ... then the trouble started ....

Regina Leader-Post, *29 September 1931*

Right, Estevan Riot, 29 September 1931: fire brigade connecting hose to use against strikers

Below, George H. Williams, President of the United Farmers of Canada (Saskatchewan Section) addressing a farmers' picnic at St. Walburg, 1930. This farmers' organization was formed in 1926 by an amalgamation of the Saskatchewan Grain Growers' Association and the Farmers' Union of Canada.

What would be my advice to you in these times of trial? . . . I believe that the greatest reason why we farmers have never got very far along the road is because we did not know which road we wanted to travel, . . . we must decide whether we are really going to accept as our road, the road to a social commonwealth, or continue to support a system of individualism and worship at the shrine of personal gain. Self or Society? Individual wealth or commonwealth? Which road? . . .

My friends, you have a right to the possession and enjoyment of the homes you have built. You have a right to a living from the fruits of your labour. You have a right to give your children the kind of future you planned for them when you brought them into this world.

George H. Williams, address, 1931[71]

Right, politics in the thirties. During the 1930s a number of parties sought the support of the electorate in the two general elections of 1934 and 1938, including two new parties, the Farmer-Labor Group (C.C.F.) formed by an amalgamation of the Political Directive Board of the United Farmers of Canada (Saskatchewan Section) and the Independent Labor party, and the Social Credit party which moved in from Alberta.

The political parties which emerged during the thirties were attempts to meet the economic crisis. Of all the people in Canada, the farmers in Saskatchewan were perhaps hardest hit by the depression, for they suffered most from drought, wheat rust, and insects.

Left, an Anderson cart, place unknown, 1937. The carts were named after Premier J. T. M. Anderson.

'Anderson carts' are pressing the 'Bennett buggies' for popular favor on Saskatchewan farms.
    Really the only difference is that the buggies have four wheels and the carts have only two.
    The buggies are really wagons and are far better than the old farm wagons, easier hauling, easier to ride in and do not have to be greased so frequently.

Regina Daily Star, *22 June 1933*

Right, a Bennett buggy along a drifted roadway, place and date unknown

That year . . . 1931, things did not improve but grew progressively worse. . . . The term "Bennett buggy" began to be heard on the farm. The [automobile] body, with motor and innards removed, just the frame left, a little blacksmithing for a hitch, a pole and the farmers had a vehicle on rubber, horse drawn which would have been much appreciated in horse and waggon days.

S. Richard, reminiscences[72]

Below, farmers picking up grasshopper poison, Indian Head, June 1939

The farmers could not control the drought but they put up a very strong fight to try to control the hordes of grasshoppers that were eating every green stalk of grain or grass in the country. They spread hundreds of tons of poisoned saw dust over their fields and road allowances early in the morning so that it would be there for the hoppers to eat when the temperature would be right for feeding.

J. A. Capling, reminiscences[73]

Right, moving from Morse to Carrot River. July 1934. Drought in the southern part of the province forced many farm families to seek new homes to the north, where land still had to be cleared and broken.

A large number of newcomers have been arriving and settling in the surrounding districts [Shell Lake] during the past week.... The real pioneer spirit was shown by one farmer who passed through ... leading a small milk cow of doubtful ancestry that was hitched with home-made harness between rough pole shafts to a cart constructed of two large wheels that upheld a horse rake.... Many hardships are encountered by these newcomers who have been arriving almost every day from less fortunate districts in the south.

Saskatoon Star-Phoenix, *22 October 1932*

Below, brush clearing equipment used in northern Saskatchewan, 1936.

Upper right, berry pickers, place unknown, about the 1930s

We escaped the drought, dust storms and grasshoppers of the prairies and we always had enough to eat, though sometimes there wasn't much variety. In the summer, we picked and canned wild raspberries, strawberries, cranberries, saskatoons and blueberries. . . . Our gardens usually provided plenty of vegetables and they kept well in those old 'dirt cellars', without a furnace. In the early summer, we cooked pigweed (lamb's quarters) and I think it tasted better than spinach. We ground wheat for porridge and roasted ground wheat or barley for coffee.

Doreen Mowery, essay[74]

Lower right, haying in the Erwood district, 1933. The family bought a team of horses but one died of swamp fever. The neighbor teamed up his dark horse with the family's gray horse to put up hay.

The change from prairie wool hay in the south to slough hay in the north was terribly hard on the cattle and horses. . . . Then the swamp fever came in . . . and they just died off something terrible. We lost most of them. . . . They come from the prairies and come into this country, into the sloughs. It was too big a change for them. It was rough on animals and people also.

David Giesbricht, reminiscences[75]

Left, listing, place and date unknown. In 1935 the Dominion government passed the Prairie Farm Rehabilitation Act to assist farmers to reduce the destructive effects of drought and soil drifting. Before the lands could be brought back to production, soil drifting had to be stopped. One of the techniques used was "listing," which consisted of gouging deep furrows and seeding them to grain or grass. The detailed development of the rehabilitation program involved the co-operation and work of a number of Dominion and provincial agencies and the dedicated work of many individuals.

Below, a farm dugout, place and date unknown. Many dugouts were constructed with the assistance of Prairie Farm Rehabilitation services to provide a supply of water for farm livestock.

Diets for Unemployment Relief

As Approved by Saskatoon Civic Relief Board
August 31, 1933

One Adult Person....................Diet 8
Man and Wife..........................Diet 16
Man and Wife with one Child
   up to two years of age......Diet 17
Man and Wife with one Child
   over 2 and under 6 yrs...Diet 17A
For each Child over 6 years
   and under 12 years of age
   add 2 diets.

For each Child over 12 years
   and under 21 years of age
   add 4 diets.

Widow or Widower and eld-
   est Child—classed.............Diet 16
   and other children as set
   out above.

NUMBER 8 DIET

Tea, Coffee or Cocoa............⅛ lb.
Sugar ....1 lb.
Butter ....½ lb.
Rice, Tapioca, Rolled Oats,
   Granules or Flour........2 lbs.
      or 1 lb. each of any two
Vegetables ....3 lbs.
      or 2 lbs. beans
      or 2 lbs. split peas
Prunes or Figs....................1 lb.
Tomatoes or Corn...............1 tin
      or ½ lb. butter
Laundry Soap.....................1 bar
Matches ....(Small) 1 box
Apples ....2 lbs.
Potatoes ....5 lbs.
Milk ....4 pts.
Meat, Fish, Eggs or Milk........30c
Bread ....4 lvs.
      or 6 lbs. flour and yeast

Per Month

Salt ....1 bag
Pepper...............................½ oz.
Baking Powder....................4 oz.
Toilet Soap (pkg. of 3).........1 pkg.

DIET 16

Tea, Coffee or Cocoa............¼ lb.
Sugar ....2 lbs.
Butter ....1 lb.
Rice or Tapioca...................2 lbs.
   or 1 lb. sugar
   or ¼ lb. tea, coffee, cocoa
R. Oats, Granules or Flour.....3 lbs.
Vegetables ....4 lbs.
      or 2 lbs. beans
      or 2 lbs. split peas
Prunes or Figs....................1 lb.
Canned Tomatoes or Corn.....1 can
      or ½ lb. Butter
Soap (Laundry) ....1 bar
Matches ....(Small) 1 box
Fresh Fruit ....(Apples) 3 lbs.
Potatoes ....10 lbs.
Meat, Fish, Eggs or Milk........50c
Milk ....7 pts.
Bread ....7 lvs.
      or 12 lbs. flour and yeast

Per Month

Salt ....1 bag
Pepper...............................1 oz.
Baking Powder....................6 oz.
Toilet Soap (pkg. of 3).........1 pkg.

Cities were not immune from economic difficulties. Many urban residents found themselves unemployed and in need of relief. Heavy social burdens fell on city governments as the numbers in need soared.

Left, relief diet, Saskatoon, August 1933

Upper right, the Saskatoon Riot, 9 May 1933. The riot developed when Saskatoon City Police and Royal Canadian Mounted Police attempted to transfer fifty of the single unemployed men housed at the Saskatoon Exhibition Buildings to another camp. Inspector L. J. Sampson of the R.C.M.P. died as a result of injuries sustained when he fell and was dragged by his horse.

Lower right, relief project, Broadway Bridge, Saskatoon, 1932: pouring concrete for the street railway tracks. The total estimated cost of the bridge, $850,000, was met by the City of Saskatoon, the Dominion government, and the Province of Saskatchewan.

Saskatoon Star-Phœnix **Evening**

VOLUME LX.—No. 245.   18 PAGES   SASKATOON, SASK., TUESDAY, MAY 9, 1933   PRICE ON TRAINS 5 CENTS

POLICEMAN DIES AFTER FIGHT WITH UNEMPLOYED

RIOTERS APPEAR IN COURT

CORONER'S JURY SWORN IN TO PROBE FATAL INJURIES SUSTAINED BY INSPECTOR

28 Men Arraigned in City Police Court This Morning on Rioting Charges; Remanded to May 17

The Prisoners

Arraigned in police court this morning on a charge of being rioters, under Sections 88 and 89 of the Criminal Code, an offense that renders them liable to two years' imprisonment with

SEARCH FOR C. L. WILLIAMS

As Police And Jobless Clashed

GREAT BRITAIN AND U.S. NOW NEAR AGREEMENT FOR TRUCE ON TARIFFS

Premier Ramsay MacDonald Tells House There Is Every Prospect of Reaching Accord on Roosevelt Proposal

Upper left, riding the rods, 1931

On the Saturday night of April 15 [1932] my friend and I took the last street car out to Sutherland having previously found out that a freight train was leaving for Winnipeg during the early hours of Sunday morning. We slunk around the yards ... Even I, with 2 pairs underclothing, 2 shirts, a sweater, my brown suit, overalls, overcoat, winter cap and 2 pairs sox was getting chilly. ... Observing the "bull" walking down the side of the train we waited till he rounded the end before ourselves, hopping out, walked after him and inspected the box cars. All but one were sealed, this "one" being half full of coal. There were already about ten other travellers sprawling in various positions amongst the coal.

Anonymous[76]

Lower left, unemployed drifters, place unknown, 1931

Towards late afternoon we arrived at the yards, parked ourselves on the grass outside the fencing and built a fire of old ties — and commenced a 7 hour wait. ...

As time passed more "travellers" appeared and settled around our fire; soon we had about a dozen fellow "unionists" and grew to discussing "this world of ours" as men often do. ...

The depression, the railway companies and Bennett were our chief topics. We wisely listened to each others views on depression. Its [sic] due to tariffs, to immigration, the price of wheat, the U.S.A., Russia, war, their "big-bugs", religion, the "bohunks". Nothing but war will bring back prosperity; no cancellation of war debts; no socialism; no God; — let's have the good old days; scrap machinery, to hell with motor cars, deport the Reds, deport the "bohunks", oust Bennett. ...

Anonymous[77]

Upper right, blanket inspection, relief camp, Dundurn, July 1933

As a measure designed to care for single homeless men without present employment and in need of relief, the department of national defense has been entrusted with the organization of a series of projects on works to the general advantage of Canada. ...

The conditions under which these works will be carried out are as follows:

Accommodation, clothing, food and medical care will be provided in kind, and an allowance not exceeding 20 cents per diem for each day worked will be issued in cash.

Eight hours per day will be worked; Sundays and statutory holidays will be observed. ...

Personnel will be free to leave the work to accept other employment offered. ...

No military discipline or training will be instituted. ...

Western Producer, *18 May 1933*

Lower right, ready to leave for work, relief camp, Dundurn, August 1934. The men were employed on the local roads and at a gravel pit.

RP 44 27 (July 1933)

RP 44-177
(August 1934)

Charter of Relief Camp Trekkers.

1 That work with wages be provided at a minimum
rate of 50 cents for unskilled labor;union
rates for all skilled work.Such work to be on
basis of five day week,six hour working day
and minimum of 20 days work per month.

2 All workers in relief camps and Goverment
Projects be covered by the Compensation Act.
Adequate first aid supplies on all relief jobs.

3 That democratically elected committees of relief
workers be recognized by the authorities.

4 Relief Camps to be taken out of the control the
Department of National Defence. No military control or
training in the relief camps.

5 A Genuine system of Social and Unemployment Insurance.
in accordance with the provisions of the Workers Social
and Unemployment Insurance Bill.

#.6 That all workers be guaranteed their democratic right to
vote.

Conditions in the relief camps were far from satisfactory from the men's point of view. The camps tended to be isolated, and the wages paid for what was often menial labor were very low. The "On to Ottawa Trek" was organized in British Columbia camps with the idea of taking the unemployed, single men's grievances and demands for improved conditions directly to Prime Minister Bennett. Their demands were incorporated into the accompanying "charter." More than 1,000 men left Vancouver and that number grew to 1,800 by the time they reached Regina. The federal authorities ordered the trek halted in Regina on 14 June but allowed the leaders to go to Ottawa to meet with Mr. Bennett. The prime minister rejected the trekkers' demands. On 1 July, a combined Regina City Police and Royal Canadian Mounted Police force attempted to arrest the leaders while they were reporting to a large gathering of strikers and sympathizers in the Regina Market Square. The resultant riot left one local policeman dead and scores of police, trekkers, and citizens injured. The strikers were subsequently dispersed, ending the "On to Ottawa Trek."

Upper left, charter of Relief Camp Trekkers, 1935

Lower left, the "On to Ottawa Trek," June 1935

Right, the Regina Riot, 1 July 1935

The depression was lifting as Their Majesties, King George VI and Queen Elizabeth made a tour of Canada in the summer of 1939. Another trial — the war — was already emerging on the world horizon. Demonstrations of loyalty and affection greeted the royal couple as their train stopped in many Saskatchewan centers.

Left, King George VI and Queen Elizabeth meeting veterans of the Riel Rebellion of 1885 during their visit to Saskatoon, 3 June 1939. Immediately to the right of the King is Carl Niderost, Mayor of Saskatoon. The veterans (left to right) are Wilfrid Latour, John Pambrun, Thomas Swain.

Right, the Royal train at Biggar, 3 June 1939

Commencing at a very early hour on Saturday morning those intending to see the King and Queen at Biggar started to take to the highways and by 8 o'clock there was a steady stream of traffic going north from Rosetown on No. 4 Highway....

At the CNR station at Biggar a number of small buildings and sheds had been removed and the number of boxcars in the yard reduced to a minimum providing a vantage point from which many viewed the proceedings.... a couple of hours before the Royal train was due an immense throng was already in place, being added to as time went on.

Rosetown Eagle,
8 June 1939

CHAPTER 7

CANADA DECLARES WAR ON GERMANY

HIGH SCHOOL COURSES

Official Information

Parents and pupils would be well advised to consult the principals in regards to collegiate and high school courses. The options available to students make this almost necessary.

Grade IX pupils in Regina, Saskatoon and Moose Jaw, and larger centres, have the opportunity of choosing one of several courses: a course leading to the normal school or the univerity; a general, a commercial or a technical course. Many of the high schools cannot offer complete commercial or technical courses, although they are introducing one or more of such sobjects.

Trustees and teachers should carefully consider the needs of the pupils when determining the subjects to be taught. Many students have no intentions of seeking entrance to normal or university, and may find it more advantageous to take the general course.

Compulsory subjects in this course are English, history and health; the optional subjects, arithmetic, algebra, geometry, general science and agriculture, art, music, home economics, Latin, French, German, book-keeping, shorthand, typewriting, house carpentry and joinery, drafting, electricity, metal work, motor engineering, and general shop work.

The Dominion of Canada for the first Time in Her History Declared War Against another State---Germany, on Sunday Last.

The Government carried out this order by the Canadian Parliament which had been summoned on Thursday, September 7th to consider the issues of war and peace. The declaration was over the signature of His Majesty King George VI.

Canada in acting on her own behalf in the matter was carrying out the authority of a Sovereign State, conferred upon her as an independent unit of the British Commonwealth of Nations. In issuing the Declaration of War Canada came under the regulations of the United States Neutrality Act, preventing her from obtaining the armaments of war from that country for herself or another country.

During the sessions of the Dominion Parliament considering it's course in the war which Britain is waging, the leaders of the four leading parties in the Commons set forth their views as to the role Canada should play. Premier King advocated volunteer enlistment for service for the defence of Canada or for overseas action, but asserted the present Government would not enact conscription.

Conservative Leader Manion while assuring the unanimous support of his party to the Government in

---

TROOPS TO GET MORE PAY THAN IN 1914

The pay of Canadian troops on active service is higher today than in 1914. Instead of $1.10 a day paid during the Great War, soldiers of the non-permanent militia now being called out on active service will receive $1.30. This rate was announced by the Defence Department on Friday.

This is the pay of private soldiers. If he has dependents the additional amount payable to his wife (or female relative who has been responsible for the care and management of his home prior to enlistment) is $35 a month. For each dependent child the soldier will receive an allowance of another $12 a month.

The dependents' allowance is contingent upon the soldier assigning $20 a month of his own pay to his wife, or to the female relative who has cared for his home.

A dependent son is eligible for the $12 a month up to the age of 16 and a dependent daughter up to the age of 17. These limits do not apply, however, in the case of a child unable through physical or mental infirmity to provide for his

The Second World War

In September 1939, just when it appeared that the end of the years of drought and depression were in sight, Canada again found itself at war. Once more Saskatchewan men and women were recruited for the armed forces and for wartime industry. Saskatchewan became a major training area for Commonwealth airmen. While the outbreak of the Second World War did not produce the same heavy demand for wheat that had occurred in 1914, there was a farm labor shortage. Many consumer items were rationed. Toward the end of the war, Saskatchewan elected the first socialist government in Canada. When the citizen armed forces were disbanded after the war, Saskatchewan's men and women returned to a province that had emerged from the depression with a buoyant, expanding economy.

Left, *Kerrobert Citizen*, 13 September 1939. On 10 September 1939, the Canadian Parliament, in an emergency session, independently declared war on Germany, and Saskatchewan was soon deeply involved in the Canadian war effort.

Below, practice-firing with a bren gun, place and date unknown. The light machine gun was an important infantry weapon, and the bren gun became familiar to thousands of Canadian soldiers.

Right, winter training exercise, Dundurn, 1941. In preparation for possible winter warfare, some troops underwent special training in the use of skis and camouflage.

Upper left, a graduation ceremony of Number Five Bombing and Gunnery School, Dafoe, 1941. Under the British Commonwealth Air Training Plan signed in 1939, Canada agreed to train air crews from Commonwealth countries. Because of its open prairie landscape, Saskatchewan became an important training center, with fifteen schools throughout the province. Training was provided for pilots, observers, navigators, wireless operators, bombardiers, and air gunners.

Lower left, mechanics in front of a Tiger Moth training aircraft, Number Six Elementary Flying Training School, Prince Albert, 1940

Upper right, assembling guns, Regina Industries Limited, date unknown. While Saskatchewan possessed limited industrial capacity many of its manufacturing plants were involved in war production. Regina Industries, a former General Motors plant, eventually had a staff of 600 employed in the manufacture of guns and gun parts.

Lower right, flight eighteen, wireless trainees, Saskatoon Technical Collegiate Institute, date unknown

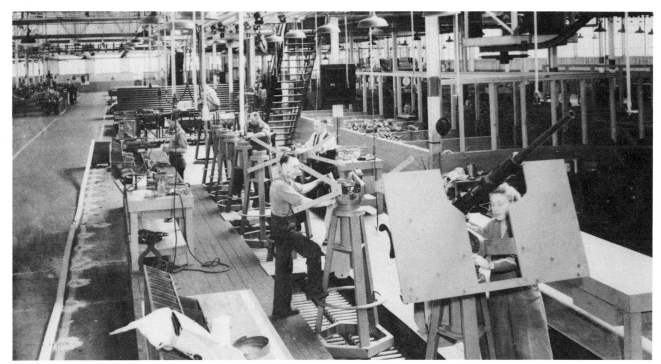

Left, men of the Saskatoon Light Infantry (M.G.), United Kingdom, about 1941

Right, Tableau of Four Freedoms at Saskatoon's fourth Victory Loan campaign demonstration, Kiwanis Park, 9 May 1943. The tableau depicted basic human freedoms proclaimed by the United Nations. The parade and tableau exhibition were intended to awaken the citizens' sense of financial obligation in supporting the men who were fighting overseas to maintain these principles.

Left, rationing was a part of wartime life at home.

Below, newspaper headlines. During the period immediately before 16 June 1944, the Third Canadian Infantry Division, which included the Regina Rifles, was engaged in the heavy fighting west of Caen, France. D-Day (6 June 1944) and the fighting in Normandy were the prelude to the massive land battles which led to the liberation of western Europe by Allied troops. Saskatchewan members of the Canadian armed forces elected three representatives to the Legislative Assembly in a special Active Service vote held in October 1944.

Weather Forecast
CLOUDY, SHOWERS

Saskatoon Star-Phœnix

Rye Close
Winnipeg:
July 108b Oct 105½b Dec 105½b

VOLUME LXXI.—No. 244.   20 PAGES   SASKATOON, SASK., FRIDAY, JUNE 16, 1944.   PUBLISHED AT 3.00 P.M.   ◆ PRICE 5 CENTS

TANK BATTLE NEAR CAUMONT

American Troops Drive Forward

SUPREME HEADQUARTERS, Allied Expeditionary Force, June 16 (CP).—British forces thrusting south from Caumont, 14 miles south of Bayeux, encountered German troops in force two miles south of the village, headquarters announced today.

Headquarters said late in the day that tank battles still raged around Tilly Sur Seulles, east of Caumont, and the city of Caen, farther east on the Orne River.

American troops attacking west of Carentan have advanced from 2½ to three miles toward the west coast of the Cherbourg peninsula, the Allied command announced.

WEATHER IS BAD

Another American column drove to within 2½ miles east of the road junction of St. Sauveur.

The weather was worse than any since D-Day with a strong wind of more than 20 miles an hour blowing from the northwest onto the beaches.

A navy officer returning from an inspection of the beachhead said the U.S. battleships Texas and Nevada were supporting American troops driving across the Cherbourg peninsula. He described American navy casualties as "very, very small."

APPROACH ST. SAUVEUR

The American thrust farther south reached to within three miles of the key road junction of St. Sauveur and within six miles of another vital communications centre, Le Haye Du Puits.

Pushing westward from Ste. Mere Eglise, one American column has reached Reigneville, three miles from St. Sauveur, where the main Paris-Caen-Bayeux-Cherbourg highway meets another highway to

can forces engaged German armor and infantry in fierce fighting six miles east of Le Haye Du Puits, on the west coast highway. Capture of this town would sever all roads on the bitterly-contested peninsula.

SEND IN RESERVES

The Germans threw reserves into the battle in this sector and bitter fighting was in progress with the front line fluctuating back and forth at frequent intervals.

C.C.F. SWEEPS PROVINCE

PICTURE OF THE WEEK—With their convoy plowing steadily toward the beaches of France, and thousands of men keyed up with excitement, these two lads calmly sleep the sleep of the just aboard their invasion craft. When the photographer took this picture they were only three miles from the shores of France. He awoke them so they could climb into their battle equipment for the D-Day landings. Pte.

SOVIETS BREAK NEW FINN DEFENCE LINE

MOSCOW, June 16 (AP).—The Red Army has smashed its way through Finland's "new Mannerheim Line," one of the last barriers on the way to the important seaport of Viipuri, it was reported today.

HUGE FORTIFICATIONS

A Red Star dispatch said the new Mannerheim Line was a tremendous fortification, with four lines of walls made of cone-shaped stone and anti-tank blocks almost two yards high, before which lay an anti-tank mine field 20 yards wide and strewn with German mines.

A great gap has been cut in this

SOVIETS
Continued on Page 2, Column 7

By Canadian Press Staff Writer

REGINA, June 16.—The first C.C.F. Government in history sailed into power on a blizzard of votes in Saskatchewan Thursday.

The vote left no more than a corporal's guard of the Liberal administration headed by Premier W. J. Patterson, provincial Premier since 1935. T. C. Douglas of Weyburn, a former member of Parliament, will head the new C.C.F. Government.

The election was one-sided from the start. Early returns showed C.C.F. candidates piling up large majorities, and then the series of individual C.C.F. successes turned into a landslide.

PATTERSON UNCERTAIN

Mr. Patterson had a small majority in his home constituency of Cannington, but could not be sure of a seat in the new Legislature until the votes cast by service men and women in Saskatchewan are counted on June 19.

Seven of his Cabinet ministers sought re-election. Five were defeated. One, Hon. T. E. Procter, Minister of Highways, was re-elected. Maj. the Hon. E. M. Culliton, minister without portfolio, ran second to a C.C.F. candidate in Gravelbourg but there was the possibility his position would be improved when the soldier vote was counted.

357,091 VOTES CAST

When the Legislature was dissolved on May 10, the Liberals had 33 seats, C.C.F. 10, Social Credit

two, Unity (National Reform) two and five were vacant.

With 438 polls still to be heard from, a compilation showed 357,091 votes had been cast Thursday, with the C.C.F. obtaining 187,437; Liberals 126,878; Progressive Conservatives 41,133 and all others 1,543.

In the last Provincial election in 1938, the total vote was 440,273, with the Liberals securing 200,376, Conservatives 52,366 and C.C.F. 82,568.

The victory was paralleled only by that of the Liberals in 1934 when they elected 50 members to the Legislature which then had 55 seats compared with the present 52.

Hon. Charles Agar, speaker in the last Legislature, was defeated.

NO PROG. CONS.

Rupert D. Ramsay, Progressive Conservative provincial leader, suffered personal defeat in Saskatoon and not one of the 40 members of his party seeking election was successful.

Voting will be held on June 26 for the remote constituency of Cumberland, where a member will be chosen from Liberal, C.C.F. and Progressive Conservative candidates to complete the Legislature

Pilotless Planes Raid England

Left, "Victory in Europe": George Baker with the *Regina Leader-Post* Extra, 7 May 1945

Upper right, the South Saskatchewan Regiment returns home to Weyburn, 24 November 1945

The train was due to arrive at Weyburn at 10.30 hours and by that time a last polish had been given to all brass and leather, ready for the last parade. The train pulled into the station where thousands of cheering people voiced their welcome. After arrival, one half hour was allowed for hellos to wives, sweethearts and families, before the regiment fell in for the big parade. The March Past was led by the S. Sask. R.'s own band under Sgt. Munday, through 15,000 wildly shouting, cheering crowds, through streets hung with banners, decorated store windows and lamp-posts with placards of the regiment's battles, to the Canadian Legion Hall where the Salute was taken by Mayor Joe Warren.

Lt. Col. G. B. Buchanan,
The March
of the Prairie Men[78]

Lower right, Victory in Europe, Navy Day, Dinsmore, 14 June 1945

Below, combining on the farm of J. B. Francis, Sedley, August 1949

Peace in 1945 marked the end of one era and the beginning of another. Saskatchewan men and women who had served throughout the world in the armed forces and who had survived the horrors of war returned to a province that had emerged from the economic depression of the thirties. Changing economic conditions, large-scale mechanized farming, new technologies and industries, modern patterns of transportation, increased urbanization, and new social concepts changed the face of Saskatchewan as it had been known by previous generations. The story of post-war development remains to be told, but the self-propelled combine symbolizes many of the features of the new era which began in 1945.

Notes

1. Jefferson, Robert, *Fifty Years on the Saskatchewan* (Battleford: Canadian North-West Historical Society, 1929), p. 58.

2. Harmon, Daniel William, *A Journal of Voyages and Travels in the Interior of North America* (Andover: Flagg and Gould, 1820), p. 81.

3. Houston, C. Stuart, ed., *To the Arctic by Canoe, 1819-1821. The Journal and Paintings of Robert Hood, midshipman with Franklin* (Montreal: The Arctic Institute of North America, McGill-Queen's University Press, 1974), pp. 74-75.

4. W. E. Traill to his mother, from Fort Ellice, 22 June 1865, W. E. Traill Papers, Saskatchewan Archives Board (hereafter SAB), Saskatoon.

5. Canada, Sessional Papers, 28, vol. 21, no. 17, *N.W.M.P. Annual Report,* "Report of Superintendent A. B. Perry at Prince Albert," 1887, p. 73.

6. See Hudson's Bay Company Archives, A.74/9/, p. 15.

7. Pelly, Joe, *A History of Cumberland House 1774-1974* (Cumberland House: Bicentennial Committee, 1974), p. 12.

8. In 1908, the Department of the Interior assigned to Frank J. P. Crean the task of procuring all information possible on the land lying to the east of the Beaver River and Green Lake, south of Churchill River, and extending east to the old canoe route from Cumberland House via Frog Portage. The object of the study was to ascertain the value of the area for farming, lumbering, and mining purposes. The work, which resulted in a comprehensive report, was completed in 1908-1909. While undertaking the survey Mr. Crean took a number of photographs, which he developed in the field. The two pictures included here give some idea of the people and landscape of northern Saskatchewan at that time.

9. Rev. John Alexander Mackay Journal, Stanley Mission, 1870-1872, in Innes Papers, SAB, Saskatoon.

10. Regina Leader, 25 October 1883.

11. Niels Gording Remembrances, SAB, Regina

12. Weston, Thomas Chesmer, *Reminiscences Among the Rock in Connection with the Geological Survey of Canada* (Toronto: Warwick Bros. and Rutler, 1899), pp. 179-180.

13. Edward Ahenakew quoted in Buck, Ruth Matheson, "The Story of the Ahenakews," *Saskatchewan History,* vol. XVII, no. 1, 1964, pp. 12-13.

14. Bryce, G., *Holiday Rambles Between Winnipeg and Victoria* (Winnipeg: no publisher, 1885), p. 57.

15. Department of the Interior, Dominion Lands Branch, file 41345, SAB, Saskatoon.

16. G. W. V. Yonge Papers, SAB, Regina.

17. Canada, Sessional Papers, 25, vol. 38, no. 10, *Department of the Interior Annual Report,* 1904, pp. 12-13.

18. William Hutchinson Diary, quoted in Lyle, G. R., "Eye Witness to Courage," *Saskatchewan History,* vol. XX, no. 3, 1967, p. 83.

19. Collingwood, Herman, "My Life History from 1904 to 1970 in Saskatchewan," SAB, Regina.

20. Smith, Hembrow F., "The Great Adventure in the North West Territory of Canada, Diary," Western Development Museum, Saskatoon.

21. *Ibid.*

22. Self, Harry, "Memoirs of My First Years in Canada as Written in 1964," SAB, Regina.

23. Davis, Charles, Glaslyn, Saskatchewan Archives Questionnaire: Pioneer Folklore, SAB, Saskatoon.

24. *Ranching in the Canadian Northwest* (no place, 1903), p. 29.

25. Stock, A. B., *Ranching in the Canadian West* (London: Adam and Charles Black, 1912), p. 36.

26. West, Edward, *Homesteading: Two Prairie Seasons* (London: T. Fisher Unwin, 1918), pp. 97-98.

27. Hutchinson, Wm., "When the Thrasher Comes," *Weekly Telegraph* (Sheffield), 7 April 1906.

28. Clark, W. C., *The Country Elevator in the Canadian West.* No. 20, Kingston: Jackson Press, 1916, p. 2.

29. Crampton, P., "Early Days in the Carrot River Valley," SAB, Saskatoon.

30. "Story of the Early Days — Hon. W. R. Motherwell, Regina," from an interview by Hopkins Moorhouse, 8 April 1916, *Saskatchewan History,* vol. VIII, no. 3, 1955, p. 109.

31. Mitchell, Sylvia, Regina, Zonta Club Essay Contest, SAB, Regina.

32. MacIntosh, Ruth, "Unforgettable Characters of Long Ago," SAB, Saskatoon.

33. Larson, Lars, Swift Current, Zonta Club Essay Contest, SAB, Regina.

34. Rodwell, Lloyd, "Saskatchewan Homestead Records," *Saskatchewan History,* vol. XVIII, no. 1, 1965, pp. 10-29.

35. Taphorn, Mrs. Minnie, "My Pioneer Days from 1906 to 1955," SAB, Saskatoon.

36. Friesen, Sarah, *Reminiscing from 1899-1916,* SAB, Saskatoon.

37. Hawthorne, Mabel (Wilson), "My Reminiscence of Fifty Years on the Saskatchewan Prairie," SAB, Regina.

38. Saskatchewan, *Public Service Monthly,* vol. II, no. 4, 1913, pp. 13-14.

39. Collingwood, Herman, "My Life History From 1904 to 1970 in Saskatchewan," SAB, Regina.

40. Cunningham, Alex, "The Biography of the Cunningham Family 1925 to 1972," SAB, Saskatoon.

41. Crampton, P., "Early Days in the Carrot River Valley," SAB, Saskatoon.

42. Gordon Bell, Vancouver, to John H. Archer, Regina, 25 May 1978, SAB, Regina.

43. Harris, G. A., "Some History and Pioneer Experiences of Heward, Sask. From its Settlement in 1900 to 1914," SAB, Regina.

44. Moore, W. T., "The Memoirs of W. T. Moore," SAB, Regina.

45. Kennedy, Allan, "Reminiscences of a Lumberjack," *Saskatchewan History,* vol. XIX, no. 1, 1966, p. 29.

46. Ouellette, Josie Olsen, "As I Recall," SAB, Regina.

47. North West Territories, Department of Agriculture, *Annual Report,* 1903, p. 142.

48. *Memories of Muenster's 70 Progressive Years, 1903-1973* (Muenster: Catholic Women's League, St. Peter's Press, about 1973), p. 17.

49. Bibbing, Mrs. W. T., "Chaplin," Mrs. W. T. Bibbing Papers, SAB, Saskatoon.

50. MacLean, Hugh, "Autobiography," Hugh MacLean Papers, SAB, Saskatoon.

51. Canada, Sessional Papers, 28, vol. 52, no. 18, *R.N.W.M.P. Annual Report,* "Report of Superintendent J. A. McGibbon at Regina," 1917, p. 27.

52. Saskatchewan, *Public Service Monthly,* vol. XIV, no. 12, 1926, p. 13.

53. Kirk, Lawrence E., "Early Years in the College of Agriculture," *Saskatchewan History,* vol. XII, no. 1, 1959, p. 29.

54. "Report to the Advisory Council in Agriculture," 18 January 1923, Dean of Agriculture, University of Saskatchewan Archives.

55. "My Experience with a Farm Truck," *Canadian Power Farmer,* vol. 26, no. 11, November 1921.

56. Canada, Department of the Interior, "Report of S.D.

Fawcett (Upper Churchill Basin of Northern Saskatchewan)," 1920, SAB, Regina.

57. Updike, Ted, "Interview on Trapping in Northern Saskatchewan," Oral History Project, SAB, Regina.

58. "Saskatchewan's First Hydro Plant," *Canadian Mining and Metallurgical Bulletin,* no. 220, August 1930, pp. 949-950.

59. Worcester, G.W., "Saskatchewan Industrial Minerals," *Canadian Mining and Metallurgical Bulletin,* no. 277, May 1935, p. 244.

60. Breed, E. *Saskatoon* (no publisher, 1913), pp. 5-8.

61. MacLean, Hugh, "Autobiography," Hugh MacLean Papers, SAB, Saskatoon.

62. Saskatchewan, Department of Highways, *Annual Report,* 1929.

63. MacKenzie, R.H., Chief Field Engineer, Department of Highways, Address to the 22nd Annual Convention of the Saskatchewan Association of Rural Municipalities.

64. "Bucking the Beautiful. Snow Bound on the Prince Albert Branch — The Singular Adventures of a Journalist," *Moose Jaw Times,* 28 April 1893, quoted in *Saskatchewan History,* vol. XIV, no. 1, 1961, pp. 30-31.

65. "Excerpts From Diary of Wm. Good, Shellbrook, Saskatchewan, 1919-1962," SAB, Saskatoon.

66. Rev. W. P. Reekie, secretary, The Social Service Council of Saskatchewan to Premier W. M. Martin, 9 January 1922, W. M. Martin Papers, p. 41363, SAB, Saskatoon.

67. Light, Alice, "My Memoirs," SAB, Saskatoon.

68. Saskatchewan, *Public Service Monthly,* vol. XIV, no. 4, 1925.

69. Canada, Sessional Papers, 13, vol. 61, no. 2, *Annual Report of the Department of Immigration and Colonization,* 1925, p. 5.

70. McIntosh, Edna Staples, interviewed by A. M. Nicholson, SAB, Saskatoon.

71. Address of George H. Williams, President of United Farmers of Canada (Saskatchewan Section), at the annual convention, 24 February 1931.

72. Richard, S., "My First Five Years In Canada — 1900-1905 and Continued to the Year 1950," SAB, Saskatoon.

73. Capling, J. A., "Would We Do It Again," SAB, Saskatoon.

74. Mowery, Doreen, Regina, Zonta Club Essay Contest, Regina.

75. Giesbrecht, David, "History of Homesteading in Northern Saskatchewan (Prince Albert)," Oral History Project, SAB, Regina.

76. "Experiences of a Depression Hobo," *Saskatchewan History,* vol. XXII, no. 2, 1969, p. 60.

77. *Ibid.,* p. 62.

78. Buchanan, Lt. Col. G. B. *The March of the Prairie Men. A Story of the South Saskatchewan Regiment* (Weyburn and Estevan: South Saskatchewan Regiment Regimental Association, 1957), p. 63.

Picture Credits

The Public Archives of Canada is abbreviated PAC.

The Saskatchewan Archives Board is abbreviated SAB. If the picture number is preceded by the letter R, it means the picture is in the Regina office. An S indicates it is in the Saskatoon office of the board.

P. xiii, George Mercer Dawson, PAC, PA 50749.

P. 2, photographer unknown, Glenbow-Alberta Institute, NA 1368-2.

P. 3, right, photographer unknown, PAC, PA 44566.

P. 3, far right, W. J. James, SAB, RA 4463.

P. 4, George Seton, watercolor, PAC, Picture Archives Branch, C 1059.

P. 5, photographer unknown, PAC, C 1716.

P. 6, photographer unknown, PAC, C 4164.

P. 7, D. B. Dowling, PAC, PA 53608.

P. 8, Frank J. P. Crean, SAB, Saskatoon.

P. 9, top, Mrs. Christina Bateman, SAB, S78-132.

P. 9, bottom, Sutherland and Company, Winnipeg, Ontario Archives, S 12771.

P. 10, top, photographer unknown, Royal Canadian Mounted Police Museum, Regina.

P. 10, bottom, D. Cadzow, Fort Battleford National Historic Park, Battleford, B.P. 170.

P. 11, William Notman, Notman Photographic Archives, McCord Museum, McGill University, No. 77,084 Misc. II.

P. 12, Thomas Chesmer Weston, PAC, PA 50835.

P. 13, Township plan, SAB, Saskatoon.

P. 14, photographer unknown, SAB, RB 990.

P. 15, photographer unknown, PAC, PA 48475.

P. 16, Department of the Interior, Dominion Lands Branch, 41345, PAC.

P. 17, photographer unknown, SAB, RA 3315, loaned for copying by the *Moosomin Spectator*.

P. 18, upper left, photographer unknown, SAB, RA 6277.

P. 18, upper right, photographer unknown, Provincial Archives of Manitoba, Riel, Louis 7.

P. 18, lower left, Hall and Lowe, SAB, RA 2872(1).

P. 18, lower right, photographer unknown, Innes Papers, SAB, RA 12850.

P. 19, upper left, photographer unknown, Osler Papers, Ontario Archives, Acc. 6876 No. 23.

P. 19, upper right, photographer unknown, PAC, C 8732.

P. 19, lower left, photographer unknown, PAC, C 2487.

P. 19, lower right, photographer unknown, Fort Battleford National Historic Park.

P. 20, photographer unknown, SAB, RB 2825.

P. 21, photographer unknown, PAC, C 1879.

P. 22, N. O. Coté, Royal Canadian Mounted Police Museum, Regina, 38-14-LXVI(d).

P. 23, Frank J. P. Crean, SAB, Sasktoon.

P. 24, photographer unknown, SAB, RA 259.

P. 26, photographer unknown, PAC, PA 21324.

P. 27, photographer unknown, Glenbow-Alberta Institute, NA 1687-37.

P. 28, photographer unknown, United Church Archives, Victoria University, Toronto.

P. 29, photographer unknown, Canadian Pacific Railway photograph, SAB, RB 3275(2).

P. 30, photographer unknown, Glenbow-Alberta Institute, NA 1368-11.

P. 31, photographer unknown, PAC, C 1311.

P. 32, photographer unknown, SAB, RA 2310.

P. 33, Rice, PAC, C 4988.

P. 34, top, photographer unknown, H. M. Jackson Photograph Collection, No. 247, SAB, S78-40.

P. 34, bottom, photographer unknown, SAB, RA 7555.

P. 35, top, photographer unknown, SAB, RA 7226(1).

P. 35, bottom, photographer unknown, Ida E. Morris photograph, SAB, S78-115.

P. 36, top, photographer unknown, Mrs. Roseland, Landrose, SAB, RA 9119.

P. 36, bottom, A. Miller album, SAB, RB 2760.

P. 37, photographer unknown, PAC, PA 48624.

P. 38, photographer unknown, Moose Jaw Public Library, Archives Department, 74-50.

P. 39, photographer unknown, Maple Creek Museum Collection, SAB, RB 9139(3).

P. 40, top, John Howard, SAB, RA 6193.

P. 40, bottom, John Howard, SAB, RA 6145.

P. 41, photographer unknown, Moose Jaw Public Library, Archives Department, 73-233.

P. 42, photographer unknown, SAB, RA 113.

P. 43, photographer unknown, SAB, RD 773(2).

P. 44, top, photographer unknown, Maple Creek Museum Collection, SAB, RB 9153.

P. 44, bottom, photographer unknown, Soo Line Historical Museum, Weyburn.

P. 45, photographer unknown, SAB, RB 1073.

P. 46, photographer unknown, Western Development Museum, Saskatoon.

P. 47, photographer unknown, Purdy photograph, SAB, S78-99.

P. 48, photographer unknown, SAB, RA 3977.

P. 49, left, photographer unknown, SAB, RA 249.

P. 49, right, photographer unknown, Saskatchewan Wheat Pool Collection, SAB, RA 15294.

P. 50, photographer unknown, SAB, RB 4195.

P. 51, photographer unknown, SAB, RB 4481.

P. 52, Rev. James A. Donaghy, Donaghy Papers, SAB, S-A42.

P. 53, top, John Howard, SAB, RA 6174.

P. 53, bottom, photographer unknown, B. H. Davidson photograph, SAB, S78-104.

P. 54, top, photographer unknown, Mrs. Margaret Salmond photograph, SAB, S79-3.

P. 54, bottom, photographer unknown, Violet McNaughton Papers, SAB, S-A1-g-12.

P. 55, photographer unknown, PAC, PA 60784.

P. 56, photographer unknown, SAB, RA 9091.

P. 57, photographer unknown, SAB, RA 4809.

P. 58, left, photographer unknown, SAB, RA 2470.

P. 58, right, E. C. Rossie, SAB, RA 3200.

P. 60, top, E. C. Rossie, SAB, RB 930.

P. 60, bottom, E. B. Curlette, Calgary, SAB, RB 1095.

P. 61, top, photographer unknown, SAB, RB 1298.

P. 61, bottom, photographer unknown, SAB, RB 18.

P. 62, photographer unknown, SAB, RA 6820.

P. 63, W. J. James, Prince Albert, SAB, RB 3676.

P. 64, top, photographer unknown, *Regina Leader-Post* photograph, SAB, RB 9073.

P. 64, bottom, photographer unknown, Moose Jaw Public Library, Archives Department, 68-342.

P. 65, photographer unknown, Western Development Museum, Saskatoon, 5-6-35.

P. 66, top, Winnipeg Photo Co., SAB, RA 3293.

P. 66, bottom, photographer unknown, *Carlyle Observer* photograph, SAB, RB 9388.

P. 67, photographer unknown, Saskatoon Public Library, Local History Room, 3270-1.

P. 68, top, photographer unknown, Glenbow-Alberta Institute, NA 2870-18.

P. 68, bottom, photographer unknown, SAB, RA 12695.

P. 69, *Grain Growers' Guide,* 7 August 1912.

P. 70, photographer unknown, Moose Jaw Public Library, Archives Department, 78-124.

P. 71, R. J. Lindsay, SAB, RB 3720.

P. 72, top, E. C. Rossie, SAB, RB 215(12).

P. 72, bottom, W. E. Veals, Veals photograph, SAB, S78-101.

P. 73, City Art Studio, Prince Albert, SAB, Saskatoon.

P. 74, photographer unknown, Western Development Museum, Saskatoon, 4-2-1.

P. 75, photographer unknown, SAB, RA 939.

P. 76, G. E. Fleming, Glenbow-Alberta Institute, NA 1368-14.

P. 77, Steele, Winnipeg, Glenbow-Alberta Institute, NA 118-33.

P. 78, photographer unknown, Moose Jaw Public Library, Archives Department, 76-35.

P. 79, photographer unknown, Moose Jaw Public Library, Archives Department, 68-311.

P. 80, top, SAB, RD 457(3).

P. 80, bottom, photographer unknown, SAB, RB 157(1).

P. 81, photographer unknown, SAB, RA 4311.

P. 82, photographer unknown, *Regina Leader-Post* photograph, SAB, RB 9074.

P. 83, top, photographer unknown, *Regina Leader-Post* photograph, SAB, RB 9072.

P. 83, bottom, photographer unknown, Saskatchewan Archives, *Star Phoenix* Collection, SAB, S 669-2.

P. 84, top, photographer unknown, Soo Line Historical Museum, Weyburn, photograph, SAB, RB 9377.

P. 84, bottom, photographer unknown, Jackson Collection, SAB, S 206.

P. 85, photographer unknown, Archives, St. Peter's College, Muenster.

P. 86, W. J. James, Prince Albert, SAB, RA 4531.

P. 87, Mr. Robinson, J.W.H. Ismond, Abernethy, photograph, SAB, RA 4912.

P. 88, photographer unknown, SAB, RB 1859.

P. 89, McKenzie, Western Development Museum, Saskatoon, 2-1-6.

P. 90, top, photographer unknown, Purdy photograph, SAB, RB 7965.

P. 90, bottom, A. H. Humphries, Melfort, SAB, RB 723.

P. 91, photographer unknown, Glenbow-Alberta Institute, NA 1095-8.

P. 92, *Regina Morning Leader,* 5 August 1914.

P. 94, *Saskatchewan Herald,* 29 July 1915.

P. 95, photographer unknown, Moose Jaw Public Library, Archives Department, 71-84.

P. 96, Johnson Art Studio, West's Studio Limited, SAB, RB 9299(c.2).

P. 97, Regina Chamber of Commerce photograph, SAB, R78-301.

P. 98, Turner Photo Studio, 30 September 1917, SAB, RB 8132(48).

P. 99, *Saskatchewan Farmer* (Moose Jaw), April 1916.

P. 100, left, *Grain Growers' Guide,* 26 February 1913.

P. 100, right, *Regina Morning Leader,* 15 February 1916.

P. 101, top, Steele, Winnipeg, SAB, RB 973.

P. 101, bottom, *Grain Growers' Guide,* 26 May 1915.

P. 102, *Kerrobert Citizen,* 14 November 1918.

P. 103, photographer unknown, Glenbow-Alberta Institute NA 2870-26.

P. 104, *Grain Growers' Guide,* 6 March 1918.

P. 105, photographer unknown, PAC, PA 22272.

P. 106, Weeks and Pugh, Moose Jaw Public Library, Archives Department, 73-96.

P. 108, *Grain Growers' Guide,* 12 January 1921.

P. 109, photographer unknown, Saskatchewan Wheat Pool Collection, SAB, RA 15263.

P. 110, photographer unknown, Saskatchewan Wheat Pool Collection, SAB, RA 15029(2).

P. 111, photographer unknown, Saskatchewan Wheat Pool Collection, SAB, RA 15020.

P. 112, *Grain Growers' Guide,* 8 January 1919.

P. 113, top, photographer unknown, University of Saskatchewan Archives.

P. 113, bottom, photographer unknown, University of Saskatchewan Archives, A 1956.

P. 114, photographer unknown, University of Saskatchewan Archives, A 1276.

P. 115, Gibson Photo, University of Saskatchewan Archives, A 1326.

P. 116, photographer unknown, Mrs. Edna Lifeso photograph, SAB, S78-95.

P. 117, photographer unknown, July 1929, *Western Producer* photograph.

P. 118, photographer unknown, SAB, RA 2260(2).

P. 119, photographer unknown, Western Development Museum, Saskatoon, 1-3-2-13.

P. 120, top, photographer unknown, PAC, PA 20171.

P. 120, bottom, photographer unknown, PAC, PA 60706.

P. 121, top, W. J. James, Prince Albert, SAB, Saskatoon.

P. 121, bottom, W. J. James, Prince Albert, SAB, Saskatoon.

P. 122, photographer unknown, PAC, PA 14002.

P. 123, photographer unknown, SAB, RA 910(1).

P. 124, top, Gibson Photo, Saskatoon.

P. 124, bottom, photographer unknown, SAB, RA 240.

P. 125, W. J. James, Prince Albert, SAB, Saskatoon.

P. 126, Capitol Art Studio, Regina, Regina Chamber of Commerce photograph, SAB, R78-301.

P. 127, Gibson Photo, Saskatoon.

P. 128, Ferguson Family Album, SAB, RA 14873(2).

P. 129, Capitol Art Studio, Regina, SAB, RA 7583.

P. 130, top, photographer unknown, SAB, RA 7534.

P. 130, lower left, photographer unknown, SAB, RA 4165(1).

P. 130, lower right, photographer unknown, SAB, RA 7748.

P. 131, top, photographer unknown, SAB, Saskatoon.

P. 131, bottom, photographer unknown, SAB, RA 7536.

P. 132, W. L. West, SAB, RB 986.

P. 133, photographer unknown, SAB, RA 9777(4).

P. 134, top, photographer unknown, SAB, RA 561(17).

P. 134, bottom, Ken Liddell, SAB, RB 2314.

P. 135, Bidwell Studio, Moose Jaw, SAB, RB 7327.

P. 136, top, W. J. James, SAB, RA 16473.

P. 136, bottom, photographer unknown, Glenbow-Alberta Institute, NA 3194-7.

P. 137, T. R. Melville-Ness, SAB, S-MN-B 2174.

P. 138, W. J. James, Prince Albert, SAB, Saskatoon.

P. 139, top, W. J. James, Prince Albert, SAB, Saskatoon.

P. 139, bottom, photographer unknown, SAB, RA 4657.

P. 140, photographer unknown, Biggar Museum and Gallery, 74.135.15.

P. 141, top, photographer unknown, Biggar Museum and Gallery.

P. 141, bottom, photographer unknown, SAB, RA 8353.

P. 142, photographer unknown, PAC, PA 88608.

P. 143, photographer unknown, Biggar Museum and Gallery.

P. 144, photographer unknown, Mrs. M. Donegan photograph, SAB, S79-13.

P. 145, photographer unknown, C. C. King photograph, SAB, S78-92.

P. 146, photographer unknown, PAC, C 43149.

P. 147, photographer unknown, PAC, PA 58806.

P. 148, photographer unknown, Mr. Joseph Bentley photograph, SAB, S78-102.

P. 149, photographer unknown, SAB, RA 5376(4).

P. 150, top, photographer unknown, PAC, C 77879.

P. 150, bottom, photographer unknown, PAC, PA 18800.

P. 151, photographer unknown, PAC, PA 88435.

P. 152, photographer unknown, PAC, PA 19079.

P. 153, photographer unknown, PAC, PA 20074.

P. 154, SAB, Saskatoon.

P. 155, photographer unknown, SAB, RA 4819(4).

P. 156, photographer unknown, Dominion Experimental Farm, Indian Head, SAB, RB 9050(1).

P. 158, photographer unknown, SAB, RA 8806(1).

P. 159, photographer unknown, SAB, RA 8806(3).

P. 160, photographer unknown, Mrs. G. H. Williams photograph, SAB.

P. 161, Political pamphlets, 1934-1938, SAB, Saskatoon.

P. 162, photographer unknown, Saskatchewan Wheat Pool Collection, SAB, RA 15072(1).

P. 163, photographer unknown, SAB, RB 1969.

P. 164, photographer unknown, Dominion Experimental Farm, Indian Head, SAB, RB 9066.

P. 165, photographer unknown, SAB, RA 4287.

P. 166, photographer unknown, H. A. Lewis Collection, SAB, RB 9258(1).

P. 167, top, photographer unknown, Miss Evelyn Ballard photograph, SAB, S78-107.

P. 167, bottom, photographer unknown, A. C. van Nes photograph, SAB, S78-110.

P. 168, photographer unknown, SAB, RA 9829.

P. 169, National Film Board photograph No. 15060, SAB, RB 8293(1).

P. 170, Pamphlet Collection, SAB, Saskatoon.

P. 171, top, *Saskatoon Star Phoenix,* 9 May 1933.

P. 171, bottom, L. Hillyard, Saskatoon Public Library, Local History Room, A 202.

P. 172, top, McDermid Studio, Ed-

monton, Glenbow-Alberta Institute, 12955(b).

P. 172, bottom, McDermid Studio, Edmonton, Glenbow-Alberta Institute, 12955(f).

P. 173, top, photographer unknown, PAC, PA 35650.

P. 173, bottom, photographer unknown, PAC, PA 35600.

P. 174, top, Royal Commission on the Regina Riot, Exhibit No. 3.

P. 174, bottom, photographer unknown, PAC, C 24834.

P. 175, top, Ken Liddell, SAB, RB 171(3).

P. 175, bottom, Ken Liddell, SAB, RB 171(1).

P. 176, *Saskatoon Star Phoenix* and L. Hillyard, Saskatoon Public Library, Local History Room, C 84.

P. 177, photographer unknown, Biggar Museum and Gallery.

P. 178, *Kerrobert Citizen,* 13 September 1939.

P. 180, photographer unknown, North Saskatchewan Regiment, Saskatoon.

P. 181, photographer unknown, SAB, Saskatoon.

P. 182, top, L. Hillyard, Saskatoon Public Library, Local History Room, C 72.

P. 182, bottom, photographer unknown, A. O. Lepine photograph, SAB, S78-118.

P. 183, top, photographer unknown, Regina Chamber of Commerce.

P. 183, bottom, photographer unknown, B. Tash photograph, SAB, SA 197.

P. 184, photographer unknown, official photograph, Canadian Military Headquarters, for general release, SAB, RB 9328(1) .

P. 185, L. Hillyard, Saskatoon Public Library, Local History Room, A 1075.

P. 186, SAB, RB 2478.

P. 187, *Saskatoon Star Phoenix*, 16 June 1944.

P. 188, photographer unknown, SAB, S78-114, Co-operative College of Canada.

P. 189, top, Charnell, Soo Line Historical Museum, Weyburn, photograph, SAB, R78-408.

P. 189, bottom, photographer unknown, Mrs. R. Stanels photograph, SAB, S78-106.

P. 190, Vern Kent, Department of Education, SAB, RB 2704(4).

Index